IMAGES
of America

WESTERN SPRINGS

ILLINOIS

The 112-foot limestone and brick water tower is the only building in Western Springs listed on the prestigious National Register of Historic Places. The tower's unusual history—it also housed the village's offices for more than 70 years—helped it achieve this national recognition. The water source was originally three springs in what is now called Spring Rock Park. They were located in the southeast portion of the park where there were soccer playing fields in 2001. Water from the springs was piped from there to the pumping station building in the park that was to the south of the in-line skating rinks. From the station, water was piped to the tower and held in the huge tank on the top floor of the tower. On August 13, 1926, the water tank sprang a leak. Thousands of gallons of water gushed down through the first and second floor offices to the basement of the tower. The tank was drained and then welded back together again.

IMAGES
of America

WESTERN SPRINGS

ILLINOIS

Betsy J. Green

ARCADIA
PUBLISHING

Published by Arcadia Publishing
Charleston, South Carolina

Library of Congress Catalog Card Number: 2002101240

For all general information contact Arcadia Publishing at:
Telephone 843-853-2070
Fax 843-853-0044
E-mail sales@arcadiapublishing.com
For customer service and orders:
Toll-Free 1-888-313-2665

Visit us on the Internet at www.arcadiapublishing.com

For many years, this post office was the center of activities in the little village of Western Springs. It originally stood at 4372 Grand Ave. Later, it was moved to 1050 W. Hillgrove Ave., between Grand and Woodland Avenues. At 5 p.m. each afternoon, a group of villagers congregated on the porch waiting for the "5 o'clock mail" to be sorted. (The mail was thrown from a passing train.) When the mail was sorted, residents filed one by one to the window and received their mail. The first Western Springs post office opened on September 12, 1873, and was probably inside a local general store. This photo was taken c. 1913. Pictured, from left to right, are Willard Lane (infant), Maude Lane, Donald Lane, Merrill Lane, Ethel Lane, William A. Collins, and Herbert Jewett. Maude Lane (the young girl on the steps) later became Maude (Lane) Erickson, one of the people to whom this book is dedicated.

CONTENTS

ACKNOWLEDGMENTS

This book is dedicated to Maude (Lane) Erickson and to the memory of Albert William Macy. Without these two, this book would not have been possible. Erickson was one of the founders of the Western Springs Historical Society and its chief archivist for many years. Most of the photos in this book have passed through her capable hands and have been saved for the enjoyment and enrichment of Western Springs residents for many years to come. Macy was the village's first historian and his scrapbook of newspaper clippings was an invaluable source of information on the village's early years.

I am very grateful for the help and fellowship of all of the Tuesday morning volunteers at the Historical Society's archives who continue in Erickson's footsteps. People who gave of their time and expertise in gathering photos and information for this book include Ann Vance, Nancy Pegram, and Betty Howard. A special thanks also to Historical Society acting president Carole Cosimano and the trustees of the society who supported my work on this book.

Unless otherwise noted, all photos are courtesy of the Western Springs Historical Society, and were digitally photographed by Connie McDonald.

Of course, the biggest thanks are due to the many residents (past and present) of Western Springs who have donated precious photographs to the Historical Society so that future generations of Western Springers will not forget the past.

Members of the Western Springs Historical Society met for the first time in 1967. Pictured from left to right are: Jill Neely, Eleanor Watts Drayer, Margaret Darrow, Kay Peter, George Darrow, Maude Erickson, Mary Virginia Rhoads, and Waldo Erickson.

INTRODUCTION

Heading southwest from Chicago, on the Burlington Northern Sante Fe train, travelers ride across the old lakebed that was formerly Glacial Lake Chicago. Roughly 14,000 years ago, this freshwater lake stretched as far west as La Grange. The first change in the land is the Tinley Moraine, a long thin stretch of rocks that was left behind by a receding glacier. The Tinley Moraine runs through Western Springs more or less from north to south. Flag Creek originally ran along the western edge of this moraine and separated it from the larger Valparaiso Moraine upon which neighboring Hinsdale was built.

There is no record of any Native-American settlement in the area where Western Springs lies today, although some stone artifacts have been unearthed in the village. Ogden Avenue and Plainfield Road, however, were originally trails used by the Indians, and there is said to have been a Native-American camp east of the county line between Ogden Avenue and Salt Creek where Bemis Woods was later established.

The earliest known land sales in the Western Springs area date to June 24 and 25 in 1835. On those two days, 10 men each bought between 40 and 160 acres in the Western Springs area for $1.20 to $1.30 per acre. Some farmed their land, while others bought it as an investment. One of the investors was Walter L. Newberry, who bought 146 acres in the northwestern portion of the village. (He later founded the Newberry Library in Chicago.) Members of the Fuller family later farmed this land. One of the buyers who farmed land in this area was Joseph Vial who purchased 80 acres where the Ridgewood subdivision is today. Sherman King bought 80 acres the next year (1836). At about this time, King built a sawmill on Salt Creek that later became the Graue flourmill.

For the next 30 years, the Western Springs area was farmed, and several farmhouses appeared on the rich prairie land. There were few trees except along Flag Creek, which was also thickly spread with reeds (also called "flags") that gave rise to its name.

In 1864, when the railroad connected the area to Chicago, the railroad company gave the area the name "Western Springs" because of the mineral springs nearby. At first, the trains carried farm produce and milk to markets in Chicago. By the 1870s, the trains carried people to the "East Hinsdale" subdivision, and the village began to take shape. Quakers and Swedish immigrants settled here, and built the first churches and a school. In 1886, the village was incorporated.

Some of the larger businesses in the village included a camera manufacturer and a nursery. Vaughan's Seed Company sold seeds and plants to help the villagers and others turn the prairie landscape into a garden suburb. The Vive Camera Company manufactured cameras that used glass-plate negatives. The business attracted numerous people with technical skills, some of whom made lasting contributions to the village in its formative years.

The village was centered around the railroad station. Wooden shops and businesses appeared nearby and also the oldest sections of the village—Old Town North and Old Town South. The 1892 water tower was also built in the heart of the village.

The village was growing by leaps and bounds in the 1920s when the village's population tripled. Schools were built on Wolf Road and Franklin Avenue. Homes began to fill the areas known as Field Park, Ridge Acres, and Forest Hills. The Police Department was organized and the Fire Department got its first fire truck.

The Baby Boom of the 1950s and then the 1960s saw homes built in the areas of Springdale, Fairview Estates, and Ridge Acres. Three elementary schools were built—Laidlaw, Forest Hills, and Field Park. The last of the farms in the village—the Dierks' farm—disappeared. The 1960s also saw the construction of the Village Hall and Police Department, the Fire Department building, and the Post Office.

The village's population of school-age children began to increase in the 1990s as younger families moved to the village. Some demolished older homes in order to build larger homes. By the year 2000, the library had increased its size, all the schools had added on, and the last large vacant section of the village—Commonwealth—saw development.

For 115 years, the village has remained a quiet community out of the limelight, nestled between its better-known neighbors of Hinsdale and La Grange. It is valued by its residents as a good place to live, to raise a family, and to spend one's retirement years. What does the future hold for Western Springs? Perhaps its past can yield some clues. Read on.

One

FOR $1.25 AN ACRE

The prairie grasses rippled over the gentle contours of the land at the edge of Cook County that stretched south of the trail (Ogden Avenue) that led from Chicago to Oswego and beyond. A grove of trees that followed Flag Creek punctuated the expanse of prairie. Mineral-rich spring water welled from the ground and fed the sloughs that dotted the landscape.

It is a small wonder that this fertile land attracted farmers from New York State where the land had been farmed out. Some came by boat along the Erie Canal to the Great Lakes. Others simply walked the entire distance. The German immigrants fled religious persecution, political turmoil, and the potato blight.

The main crop in 1850 was corn, used to feed both farm animals and people. "Milch" cows were used to produce large quantities of butter, most of which was sold. By 1880, the Dierks' family farm (in the Springdale area) grew mostly hay and produced 1,400 gallons of milk a year. These were both sold and probably shipped to Chicago by train.

Just six years later (in 1886), the people living near the railroad station voted to incorporate. When the water tower and its water system was in place in 1893, the future of the village was assured. Gradually subdivisions swallowed up the farms. Yet traces of the past remained for years in the shape of strawberry patches and large backyard gardens. "Victory gardens" created during World Wars I and II also carried on the farming tradition.

When the hay was stacked, you could climb to the top and view the surrounding farmland. In the mid 1800s, there may have been as many as four farms along the west side of Willow Springs Road between 47th Street and 55th Street. These barns and hay stacks belonged to the family of Dietrich Dierks who lived at 5160 Willow Springs Rd. (The home was later demolished.)

As the Dierks family's fortunes grew, they bought more land and hired workers to help with the farm chores. Dietrich Dierks sits on the left; the rest are unidentified. Some may be hired hands, some could be his sons. Mrs. Dierks and her daughters would have prepared the meals for all the men. Many farm wives in this area also produced hundred of pounds of butter each year to sell. The Dierks had three daughters and five sons—most of them did not marry. In 1955, Ernest and Caroline Dierks, the two remaining children, sold the farm to developers who created the Springdale Subdivision. The home's front porch faced Willow Springs Road which (along with Wolf Road) appeared on an 1851 map of the area. Ogden Avenue and Plainfield Road also existed at that early date.

This aerial view (*c.* 1920s) of the Dierks' farm shows Willow Springs Road in the lower right. The Dierks owned their land and were considered fairly prosperous. (Some of the other farmers on Willow Springs Road were tenants.) The Dierks had a large house, two frame barns, a windmill, and a milk house. Some of the trees were apple trees.

A photographer, standing in the empty field on the east side of Willow Springs Road, snapped this photo of the Dierks' homestead as it looked in 1958, about 100 years after the Dierks left their old home in Germany. The farm's windmill is clearly visible. Out of sight, to the west of the house, the first houses of the Springdale Subdivision have already appeared.

Ernest Dierks casts an admiring eye at his favorite steed. Ernest was one of the eight Dierks children. In 1955, when he was 77, he and his sister Caroline sold most of the family farm to developers who created the Springdale Subdivision. Besides horses, the Dierks' farm included cattle, *milch* cows, mules, hogs, and chickens.

Harvest work on the Dierks' farm was a busy time as the extra hired hands helped with the farm equipment. Harvesting time also meant extra work for Mrs. Dierks (Dorothea Hogreve) and her three daughters who probably prepared the meals for the men and boys who worked in the fields. According to a 1910 insurance policy, the Dierks owned reapers, mowers, harvesters, plows, cultivators, harrows, a hay press, corn shellers, and shredders.

12

Two horses pull an unidentified man on a small hay cutter on the Dierks' farm. Leather string devices on the horses' backs discouraged flies. The grassy landscape with a few scattered trees in the background was typical of what the first settlers saw when they arrived in this area in the 1840s. The Springdale area stayed this way until the 1950s.

Ernest Dierks plows between his family's apple trees. The Busching family occupied the home in the distance. The Buschings were another German immigrant family. They probably rented their farm on the west side of Willow Springs Road because their name does not appear on any farm ownership maps.

"Uncle Ed" Fuller was one of the more colorful characters in Western Springs in the late 1800s and early 1900s. He owned land in the northwest portion of the village, both north and south of Ogden Avenue. His grandfather founded Fullersburg, and Uncle Ed (Edwin C. Fuller) was born there. Fuller was a popular fiddler at the Fullersburg tavern that he managed with his brother.

Admiring baby chicks on the Fuller farm are Blanche Heinemann (left) and Marca Fuller, her foster mother. Marca was the wife of Uncle Ed Fuller. Many Western Springs residents raised chickens for their own use. Real estate ads for Western Springs in the 1920s extolled the virtues of raising chickens and growing fruit trees in one's yard.

Western Springs residents did not have far to go to visit farm animals in the early 1900s. Looking over the calves on the Ed Fuller farm, from left to right, are Leona Carter Schroeder, Amanda Lundquist Ressler, Waldo Erickson, Esther Lundquist Weigle, and Ed Fuller. Waldo later became the Western Springs fire chief.

Another farm in the Western Springs area belonged to the Durland family. Here, Margaret Louise (Unger) Durland and her daughter Anna pose for a photo while visiting still another local farm. The farm pictured belonged to the McKana family and was located on Plainfield Road. Anna later married Elmer A. McKana. The Durlands had lived in Western Springs since 1881.

Joseph Vial and his family were one of the earliest farming families to settle in the Western Springs area. In 1834, the Vials arrived from New York State, where many other early native-born settlers in this area originated. The Pottawatomie Indians were still in the area. Their first log cabin served as an inn, post office, store, and was the meeting place for Cook County's first Democratic Convention in 1836. In 1856, Joseph's son Robert Vial built a two-story frame farmhouse on Plainfield Road. In 1989, when the home was threatened with demolition, the Flagg Creek Historical Society moved the farmhouse, and spent several years restoring the home's interior and exterior. In 1999, they opened it to the public on a regular basis. Pictured, from left to right, are as follows: (front row) Mary R. (Ketchum) Vial, her husband Robert Vial, and May (Vial) Craigmile; (back row) Robert Clark Vial, Alice M. Vial, Eugene S. Vial, Edmond R. Vial, and Frederick Ketchum.

August Ekdahl was a Swedish immigrant shoemaker who settled in the village. He left Sweden in 1881, and lived in Chicago until 1886 when he moved to Western Springs. The next year, he married another newly arrived Swedish immigrant—Augusta Sophia Karlsson. August kept his cow in a barn behind the 808 Hillgrove Ave. building. In 2001, the Spaghetti House Restaurant occupied the 808 Hillgrove Ave. address.

When there was more vacant land around the village in the 1800s and early 1900s, there were several strawberry gardens. These people (more Swedish immigrants) enjoy a sunny day in Hart's Strawberry Patch near the intersection of Plainfield and Wolf roads. Pictured, from left to right, are Georgine (Durland) Olson, Margaret Louise (Unger) Hart (formerly Durland), baby Harriet Olson, Louis K. Hart, baby Lorraine ?, and Alma (Olson) Thurson.

17

Lawrence Castrodale, an immigrant from Italy, tends to two cows on the dirt road in front of a home at 4328 Prospect Ave. (later demolished). Castrodale came to Western Springs in 1893 at the age of 19 and first worked for the Vive Camera Company. He married Augusta Olson, a Swedish immigrant, and together they raised four children. Over the years, Castrodale worked as an electrical engineer and served as the village's electrician. He was also the engineer at the village's water and power plant on 47th Street where Spring Rock Park was in 2001. He installed the first wiring and telephones in many older homes here. Most homes originally had a 100-watt line running into the home—enough to power four 25-watt light bulbs. In 1913, Castrodale owned an electrical appliance shop in Western Springs and sold electrical washing machines that could be paid for in weekly installments of $1.50.

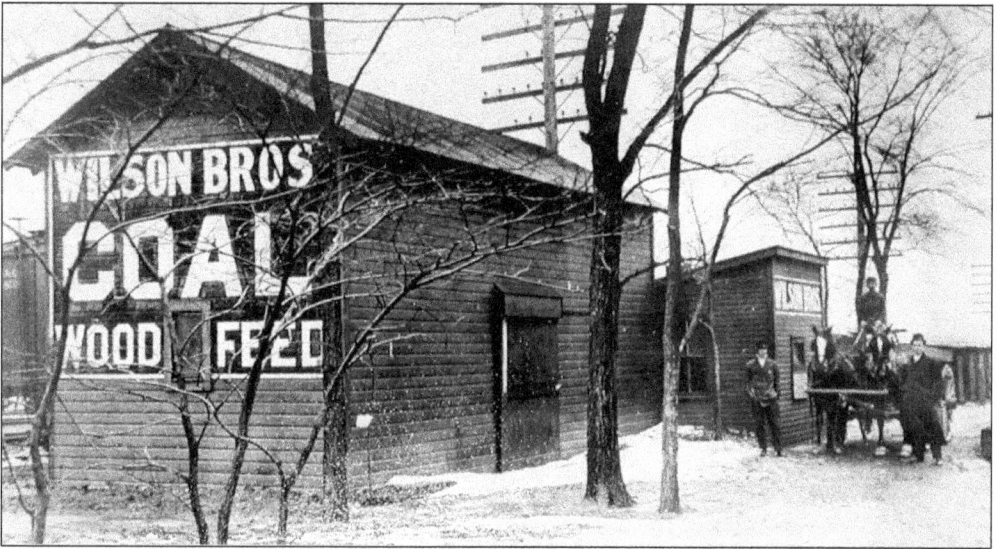

The Wilson Brothers Coal Company sold coal, wood, and chicken feed. It was located at the corner of Hillgrove and Central avenues from 1906 to 1912 (where the White Hen store was located in 2001). At the far left is a boxcar on the railroad siding. The siding was between the train track and Hillgrove Avenue, just west of Central Avenue. Coal was shoveled from a boxcar into a wagon or truck. The men are unidentified.

Many homes in the village had large gardens in the late 1800s and early 1900s. Growing your own food ensured its quality, especially before the Pure Food and Drug Act of 1906 outlawed the sale of diseased meat, decomposed foods, and dangerous food additives. Daniel A. Arnold, a Civil War veteran, tends his daughter's garden behind her home at 4364 Grand Ave. This home still existed in 2001.

This photo was taken from atop a water tank (looking west from what was the Garden Market Shopping Center in 2001). Most of the foreground is occupied by the rows of plants grown by Vaughan's Nursery. The buildings in the middle ground are greenhouses and packing sheds. John Charles Vaughan moved his seed company to Western Springs in the 1880s. The company's main offices were located on the west end of Hillgrove Avenue where the swimming pool was in 2001. In the background, past Wolf Road, the land looks as it must have looked when settlers first arrived in the 1830s—flat prairie, some trees, and a slough in the upper right. The trees in the extreme background lined Flag Creek. In the 1920s, the homes of the Forest Hills Subdivision were built west of Wolf Road.

Two

HOLIDAYS AND
EVERYDAYS

Everyday life in Western Springs was a large measure of home life, work, and school, mixed together and spiced with special occasions and holidays.

A great proportion of residents worked in the village for companies such as Vive Camera and Vaughan's Seed Company. Some residents started their own businesses in the village. Men tended to run businesses such as dry goods stores or groceries. Women managed bakeries, small restaurants called teahouses, beauty salons, or taught music.

A number of men and women commuted to offices in Chicago. They were in business, finance, law, publishing, journalism, or manufacturing. One Western Springs resident wrote for a Chicago newspaper, and later became a famous Milwaukee journalist.

Women spent many hours caring for their home and their family. Housewives spent long hours cooking on coal stoves using recipes that instructed them to judge the oven temperature by how many seconds they could keep their hand in the oven.

Children's lives focused on schoolwork. School picture day did not mean that individual color photos were taken. Instead, the whole class assembled outside and posed for a black and white group shot with their teacher. In the 1890s, there were perhaps a dozen children in each grade. By the 1920s, when the village's population skyrocketed, there were more than 35 to a class.

Everyone looked forward to holidays and special occasions. Christmas was a favorite time for young and old. One of the oldest and most visible cultural institutions was the Theatre of Western Springs. It was founded in 1929.

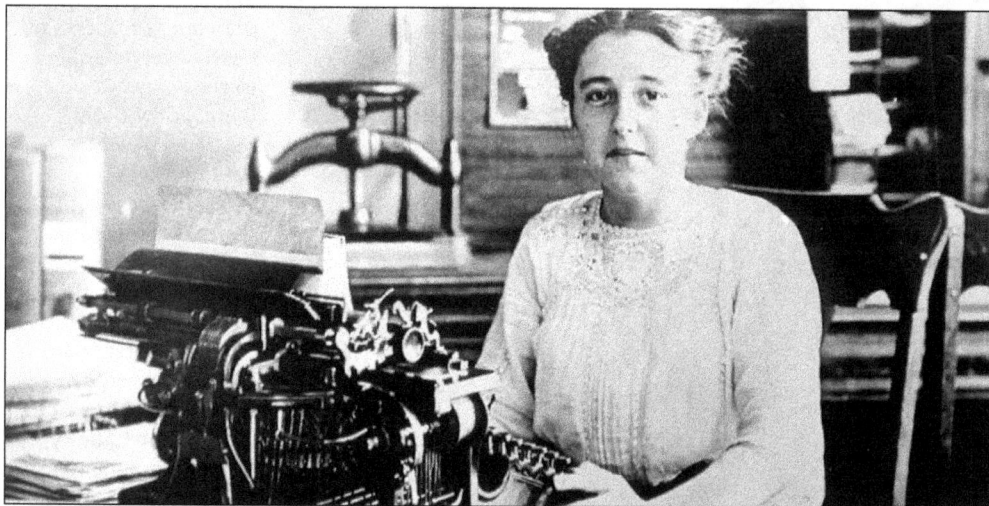

Lena Kittle (also called Kettle) sits before typewriter at her desk in the Vaughan Seed Company, one of the largest businesses in Western Springs in the late 1800s and early 1900s. Kittle's hairstyle and clothing date this photo in the first decade or two of the 1900s. Typewriters were introduced into the business world in 1874. Lena's husband George may have been a florist and probably also worked for the seed company.

Dressed as the Queen of Sheba, Western Springs journalist Ione (Quinby) Griggs was a reporter and columnist for the *Chicago Evening Post* in the early 1930s. This photo was taken when she rode on an elephant and led a circus parade in Chicago. She wrote about her experience for the newspaper. Griggs interviewed many prominent people including Amelia Earhart, Jean Harlow, and Al Capone (in his prison cell). From 1934 until she retired in 1985, Griggs wrote an advice column in the *Milwaukee Journal* newspaper. She sometimes received as many as 7,000 letters a week. Griggs was immensely popular with the paper's readers and nearly every visitor to the *Milwaukee Journal* newsroom wanted to see her. When Griggs died in 1991, her best-kept secret was revealed. She was 100 years old, and had learned to write her columns on a computer when she was in her 90s. She is commemorated by the Ione Quinby Griggs scholarship at the Journalism & Mass Communication College at the University of Wisconsin at Milwaukee.

In the years before supermarkets, women did their food shopping in groceries such as this one—the Western Springs Grocery and Market at 810 Hillgrove Ave. The customer stood at the counter and asked the store clerk to hand her the items on her shopping list. This photo appears to date from the 1930s. Pictured, from left to right, are unidentified, Eleanor Borchardt, William Borchardt, and unidentified.

The general store (sometimes called dry goods store) was another type of store in the village. Located at 917 Burlington Ave. was the General Merchandising Store owned by Herbert J. Buck. The store was an unofficial gathering place. Commuters stopped here to pick up a newspaper in the morning, and youngsters came to buy their school supplies. Pictured are Theresa Stiegerwald (left) and LeVonne Smith.

23

Western Springs businesswoman Lucy Blair owned her own Beauty Shop in the 1920s, 30s, and 40s. She advertised "finger waves," a 1930's flat-wave style created with pin curls, for 35¢. The shop was located at 4466 Lawn Ave., and at 903 Burlington Ave. at another date. The two women in the photo are Verna Freeman (left) and Lucy Blair.

Another immigrant in Western Springs at the turn of the 20th century was Gustave A. Walters, who was the manager of the leather department for the Vive Camera Company. He was born in Germany in 1848 and came to the village in the 1890s. When the camera company closed in 1905, he opened his own business in Chicago making leather cases.

Pictured here is a dramatic scene from *The Young and the Fair*—the second production of the 1949-50 season at the Theatre of Western Springs. Other productions that season (the theater's 21st year) were: *Three Men on a Horse, The Wizard of Oz, Edward, My Son,* and *The Taming of the Shrew.* The production's director, Mary Cattell, wrote in the program, "It has been our desire to bring to our community and those surrounding it the finest possible theatre entertainment in a well balanced diet of four outstanding plays each season, with an additional fillip, a play not included in the subscription, which has been carefully selected for its exceptional qualities rather than for its wide-spread and general appeal." The Theatre of Western Springs was born in the home of Mary Cattell in 1929. TWS's first production was on December 19, 1929. (Photo courtesy of the Theatre of Western Springs.)

A modern young couple prepares a meal in their up-to-date kitchen *c.* 1913. Marion Stocker Dana (left) and Walter Dana were married in 1912. According to the gossip column in the *Western Springs Times* newspaper on December 1, 1913, "Mr. and Mrs. Walter Dana moved into their new home on Woodland Ave." This photo may have been taken at that time.

Here we see Christmas morning with a candle-lit tree at the William Paine Quinby home in the early 1900s. A 1914 article in the *Western Springs Times* cautioned: "Don't leave the lighted tree unwatched. Don't let children touch the tree. Don't remove presents from the tree until the candles are extinguished. Don't permit a draft of air to sway the branches of the tree until the candles are extinguished."

Christmas (*c.* 1917) is celebrated at the home of the William Blair family. Electrical lights were becoming more common on Christmas trees. These lights were appealing because they did not create grease, dirt, or smoke. Still, they were considered dangerous and some parents forbade children to play at the homes of friends whose Christmas trees were lit by electrical lights. Pictured, from left to right, are Bessie Blair, Billy Blair, and Lucy Blair.

Christmas tree lights at the Lawrence Castrodale family's home were undoubtedly electric by 1940. This family probably had one of the first electrically-lit trees—Castrodale had been the village's electrician. Pictured, from left to right, are Lawrence Castrodale, his wife Augusta (Olson) Castrodale, Daniel Castrodale, Marian Castrodale, baby Elwood Castrodale, Ethel (Owen) Castrodale, Ella Owen, and Mary Olson.

The dining room of the Ellmore C. Patterson home at 4344 Grand Ave. is shown c. 1915. The room is decorated in the Arts and Crafts (also called Craftsman) style popular at that time. This style was much simpler than the ornate Victorian styles of interior decoration that were popular in the late 1800s. Concern about germs and disease partly influenced this simpler style that was easier to clean.

In the same house, a William Morris-inspired wallpaper was used. Built-in furniture, such as the bench under the stairs, was also popular in the Arts and Crafts movement. T.C. Hill, one of the first real estate developers in Western Springs, built this home for himself. This home still stood in 2001.

Later known as McClure Junior High School, the Wolf Road (elementary) School was built at 4225 Wolf Rd. in 1924 for $48,000. The school was named for E.P. McClure who donated the land on which the school was built. McClure served as president of the Western Springs School Board for 15 years. This view is from the southwest.

Originally known as the Franklin Avenue School and later renamed the Maurice P. Clark School, this building was built in 1939. Clark was the Superintendent of School District 101 from 1956 to 1974. The school closed in the 1980s, and later was used as the Recreation Center. It was demolished in the late 1990s.

Built in 1885, the Grand Avenue School operated as a school until 1980. The fire escape on the right was the scene of a prank in the early decades of the 1900s when a group of boys, under the cover of darkness, dragged a wooden delivery wagon up the stairs of the fire escape, and left it there for the children to discover the next morning.

In 1896, the teachers and students of the primary (kindergarten), first, second, and third grades pose for a photo outside the Grand Avenue School. Teacher Mr. B.F. Clark is on the right; Miss Merriman is on the left. Only unmarried women were allowed to teach. When a woman married, she had to retire from teaching. The students are unidentified.

Twenty-seven years later, in 1923, the second graders posed for their photos outside the school. Pictured, from left to right, are as follows: (front row) Philip Adams, Robert Morehouse, Robert Wood, Frank George Dean, Richard Johnson, Philip Paynter, Thomas Rollow, Charles Szypura, and Henry Mellbom; (second row) Elmer Fippinger, Stewart Ross, Henry Bruno, Eugene Halm, Ford Porter, Jr., Joseph Fippinger, Arthur Zitzka, Alfred Humphrey, and Clifford Lundin; (third row) Thomas Phee, Russell James Jr., Burton Clark, Muriel Reeve, Gertrude Winslow, Peggy Knocke, Leona Deke, Marion Banker, Wilbur Anderson, and Roger Johnson; (back row) Martha Curtis, Mary Florence Probst, Margaret Gustavson, Lucille Bromney, Mary Helen Cattell, Kathryn Knopp, Mary Sabik, Laura Ventresca, and Frances Bear; the teacher is unidentified.

FORD MEMORIAL LIBRARY 1-102
WESTERN SPRINGS

In 1932, Eleanor (Blount) Ford donated a stone building and the property on the northwest corner of Wolf Road and Chestnut Street to be used as a library. It was named after her late husband Thomas A. Ford. As the library grew, there were several additions. The most recent was in 1992.

PUMPING STATION

Built as the Water Pumping Station, this building drew water from three spring-fed wells on the northwest corner of 47th Street and Central Avenue. The building was located in what is now the southwest portion of Spring Rock Park. Water was pumped from here to the water tower in town. When this photo was taken in 1914, this building served as the electricity-generating plant for Western Springs. It was demolished c. 1924.

Three

GETTING FROM
HERE TO THERE

People walked to get somewhere. They walked to school, to the center of town to shop or catch the train, or to visit with friends. They walked in shoes of leather or fabric, fastened with laces or buttons.

Families with more money had their own horses or ponies and a buggy, cart, or wagon. Others rented these from a livery stable. Local businesses made deliveries of fresh produce, ice, milk, or coal.

A few lucky boys or girls had their own donkey or pony. Little girls took their dolls out for an airing in doll strollers.

The train tracks of the "Q" (the Chicago, Burlington & Quincy Railroad) formed the main street of the village. Western Springs has no "Main Street." In the 1860s, only a few stops were made to pick up farmers' milk cans. In later decades, the trains stopped regularly for commuters headed into and out of Chicago. At first, bags of mail were ejected unceremoniously from express trains. Hapless passersby were sometimes rendered unconscious by this version of "speedy delivery." At other times, the mail sack would be suctioned under the train and shredded into bite-sized pieces.

About 1900, the first "horseless carriages" bucked and blustered along the dirt roads in Western Springs. A local piano teacher drove one of the earliest autos. Another villager set several long-distance driving records in Packard automobiles. Most photos show people in an open car in pleasant weather. Many early cars were put in storage for the winter.

Janet Sampson is at the wheel of a roadster. Although the car had a collapsible roof for cool or rainy weather, many cars of this vintage had their wheels removed and were put on blocks and stored during the winter months. Cars were prone to breakdowns, in part because many roads were rough or unpaved.

A Chicago, Burlington & Quincy steam train passes through the railroad station in the early 1900s. The railroad was built as a single track in 1864 and connected the village to Chicago. It was the railroad company that gave the area its name—Western Springs. Heading westward, the tracks led to Aurora, and then to Galesburg where passengers could continue on to Quincy, Illinois or Burlington, Iowa. In addition to carrying passengers and freight, the trains carried the mail to Western Springs. In the village's early years, residents would pick up mail in Chicago and carry it back to the village. Later, the train company took over this job and hurled heavy sacks of mail onto the station platform from express trains. More than one person was beaned by a bag of mail. Eventually villagers petitioned the CB&Q to carry mail only on local trains. An employee sat in the tower (seen to the left of the train) and operated the gates at the grade crossings.

Agnes Henrikson (left) and Elsie Peterson pose on a boxcar parked on the siding at Central Avenue on the north side of the tracks, south of Hillgrove Avenue *c.* 1915. Agnes' father owned the local grocery store. Peterson did not live in Western Springs, but she spent much time here visiting her cousins, the Pearsons.

Commuters board the CB&Q train to Chicago. Before Chicago's Union Station was built in 1913, trains arrived at an older structure in Chicago nicknamed "the shed." In 1909, a poem in the *La Grange Citizen* newspaper bemoaned the plight of commuters: ". . . speaking of martyrs, O, where will you find an army more noble and true than the wretches who wait for the ump-umpty-eight in the *shed* of the CB&Q."

Some lucky lads in Western Springs owned their own steed. Here, c. 1890, Herbert Cattell poses on his pet donkey. He lived at 4472 Grand Ave. (This home was later demolished.) Cattell was born in Western Springs and was active in the Village Club when he was older. His wife, Mary (Tredwell) Cattell founded the Theatre of Western Springs.

Farm owner Walter Durland rides in his buggy. Some families owned their own horse and carriage, and kept these in a carriage house at the back of their property. Others rented a horse and vehicle from a livery stable. The word "livery" was later used on the license plates of rented automobiles.

Mary Hendrickson stops by the side of the road with a horse and buggy that she and her husband Nels (also spelled Nils) owned jointly with another immigrant family—Albert and Frieda Lundin. The horse and vehicle were kept in the Hendrickson barn behind their home at 4140 Forest Ave. (This home still stood in 2001.) Nels Hendrickson worked for Vaughan's Seed Company, and also drove a delivery wagon and a *hack* (carriage for hire).

An unidentified family stands in front of a home on Willow Springs Road. This home was located south of the Dierks' home (5160 Willow Springs Rd.) on a farm belonging to the Robb family of La Grange. William Robb was one of the earliest settlers of that village.

The pony pulling Horace Stocker's two-seater wicker carriage was one of a pair named Fleet and Dewey to commemorate a victory in the Spanish-American War of 1898. The ponies were named after Admiral George Dewey and his fleet, the victors over the Spanish in the Battle of Manila in the Philippines. Pictured, from left to right, are Walter Dana, Julia Stocker, and Wilbur Anderson.

In the 1890s and early 1900s, clambakes on the banks of the Des Plaines River in a park in Lyons were popular activities. This vehicle, called a *talley-ho*, transported picnickers to the clambake in style. The coach was mahogany trimmed with brass and had red velvet seats inside. The passengers are unidentified Western Springs residents.

Stores in Western Springs delivered purchases to the homes of customers in the late 1800s and early 1900s. The J. Henrikson Grocery and Market had operated in Western Springs since about 1895. This delivery van is parked on the street in front of the water tower with the train tracks in the middle ground. The driver is Harley Perrott.

Swedish immigrant Nels (also spelled Nils) Hendrickson and his wife Mary settled in Western Springs c. 1903. In addition to their horse, they owned a cow and kept some chickens. Hendrickson operated a delivery wagon. The houses in the background were on the northwest corner of Hillgrove and Grand avenues. They were demolished in the 1930s and replaced by a gas station. In the 1990s, a bank replaced the gas station.

In 1914, Western Springs residents Ellmore C. Clark (right) and John E. Williams set a record when they traveled non-stop from Chicago to New York in this Packard auto in less than 40 hours. Roads were not well marked in the early 1900s, so Patterson had six airplanes that flew above him to guide him. Many of the roads would have been unpaved. When Patterson reached New York, he was too exhausted to get his suitcase out of the car. Patterson settled in Western Springs in 1893 and initially worked for the Vive Camera Company that had been founded by his cousin John Atwater. (The camera company attracted a number of technically talented men to the village.) He was later vice-president and general manager of Colliers magazine, and co-founder of Warner-Patterson, a company that manufactured automobile accessories. The houses in the background are at 4336 and 4332 Grand Ave. (Both still stood in 2001.)

The next year (1915), E.C. Patterson repeated his non-stop drive (in another Packard) to New York and cut his time to less than 36 hours. In addition to his own driving, Patterson owned racing cars and hired Ralph DePalma to race them. After some local successes, Patterson bought a special racing car made in Belgium by Mercedes and had DePalma race it at the 500-mile race at Indianapolis. DePalma won. Patterson turned the $2,000 prize over to DePalma. In addition to his interest in automobile racing, Patterson coached local boys in boxing for about 40 years, and founded the Western Springs Cadets, a drill squad. Patterson also appeared in numerous amateur theatricals in the village. He and his wife Harriet raised four children, plus two nephews. Ironically, this man, who was so interested in speed, was killed in 1946 at the train crossing in Western Springs by the Burlington *Zephyr*, a high-speed passenger train.

Florence Henthorne, a Western Springs piano teacher, proudly drives her car along the road. The car may be a *c.* 1905 Cadillac Model A. The company built only several thousand of these cars each year. The price for this five-horsepower car was about $750. Henthorne arrived in the village with her family in 1880 when she was five years old. She received a degree from the Chicago Musical College and taught piano for many years. She was one of the founders of the Western Springs Music Club.

This car is identified as a 1905 or 1906 Studebaker. George Allen owned the car. The Studebaker family had been making wagons and carriages in South Bend, Indiana, since the 1850s. In 1902, they produced their first *horseless carriage*. A car like this could have had a 16-horsepower engine and a price tag of about $1,600.

Motoring along in a 1914 Ford Model T Touring Car are Donald Lane (left) and his brother Merrill. This photo, however, was taken in 1921 judging from the date on the car's license plate. The Model T was nicknamed the *Tin Lizzie*. This car's gas tank was located under the passenger seat.

Helen Murphy cranks the starter on this sporty two-door coupe as Pearl Winternitz steps up on the running board. Until 1912, all American cars had to be cranked to start. The make of the car is unknown—there were more than 100 automakers in the United States in the early decades of the 1900s.

In 1931, housewives in Western Springs could call the Henrikson-Rose Grocery and Meat Company and order groceries to be delivered to their homes. Carl Neuert, here age 29, was the manager for the company and later married Agnes Elizabeth Henrikson, the boss's daughter. (Agnes appears in an earlier photo in this chapter.) Neuert was also in real estate and served as the director of a local bank.

Albert Lundin drives his company's truck. (He and his wife appear in a later chapter.) Lundin was a Norwegian immigrant who arrived in Western Springs in 1905. He married in 1909, and with his wife Frieda Mathilda (Eckstrand) (a Swedish immigrant) raised four children. Lundin was a builder-carpenter and built many homes in Western Springs. The company he founded still existed in 2001.

Dorothy Stocker takes her doll out for an airing in an elaborate doll carriage. Dorothy's father, Horace Stocker moved to Western Springs in 1892. Her father was a successful businessman who was the owner of the H.A. Stocker Machinery Company in the 1890s and early 1900s. He also found time to participate in local government. He was a village trustee from 1895 to 1898, and later village president from 1902 to 1905. Stocker was also president of the Board of Education. Dorothy was born in the village in 1901, so this photo was probably taken c. 1906. The scenery behind her was typical of Western Springs in the early 1900s—lots of empty lots. The homes (from left to right) are: 4064 Lawn Ave., 4069 Lawn Ave., and 3930 Lawn Ave. The first two homes still stood in 2001.

Boys made scooters out of wheels from metal roller skates and wooden boxes. Sometimes they raced these vehicles in *soapbox derbies*. This photo was taken in the late 1910s. Mabel Betsey (Mahaffay) Lane watches from the porch of the home at 1222 Chestnut St. (This home still stood in 2001.) The boys, from left to right, are Norman Levy, Merrill Lane, Herbert Rhoads, Ernest Bollnow, Donald Lane, and Willard Lane.

Young men preferred motorcycles. In this 1908 photo, Allen Craig (left) and Emory Patterson get ready for a ride. The Harley-Davidson Company was founded in 1903 by William Harley and three Davidson brothers. Not everyone loved motorcycles. In 1914 the village board instituted "a series of wholesome fines" against speeding vehicles on local streets.

Four

ENJOYING THE OUTDOORS

Tennis, one of the more popular sports in Western Springs in 2001, has been a favorite activity in the village for more than a century. Grass or clay courts were more common in the past when numerous families had property large enough to accommodate a tennis court. The game must have been played more sedately—men played in trousers, shirts, and jackets (sports jackets?) and women wore long skirts or dresses. Baseball was another popular sport in 1900 and 2001.

Organized outdoor activities for boys and girls began in the village shortly after 1910. The boys joined the Boy Scouts and dressed in military-inspired uniforms. The Campfire Girls took Native Americans as their model. Both groups also performed public services such as scrap drives or distributing warm clothing to the needy.

Summer days could be spent reading a good book on one's front porch or picnicking with friends in a backyard or along the banks of Salt Creek.

The creek was a popular spot for wading, swimming, and fishing. Camp Bemis, a dormitory-style cabin, accommodated Chicago children who came out for short visits. The local Scouts also built a log cabin near the creek. In the 1920s, a dam near the Wolf Road Bridge created a popular swimming hole.

In the first half of the 1900s, Western Springs youngsters had one source of outdoor fun that later disappeared—the sloughs. In the springtime, the western end of Hillgrove Avenue would flood. Kids sailed on homemade rafts. Older kids trapped muskrats.

This 1920 photo shows boys on homemade rafts in the large slough that appeared each spring on the western end of Hillgrove Avenue near the intersection of Hampton Avenue. Behind them are the greenhouses of Vaughan's Seed Company. Pictured, from left to right, are Walter Burr, Nelson Nealy, and Charles Vaughan. In addition to the boys, muskrats also enjoyed this area.

Christine "Mama" Johnson and her foster daughter Minnie stand behind their home at 4473 Woodland Ave. (This home was later demolished.) Johnson with her husband Andrew settled in Western Springs in 1873 just a few years after leaving their native Sweden. Christine was a midwife, and ran a bakery and a boarding house where newer Swedish immigrants stayed until their financial situation improved. A deeply religious woman, she and other immigrants began holding worship services in her home. Later, she mortgaged her house to help raise funds to build the Swedish Methodist Church at 1215 Chestnut St. This church was built in 1893 and held worshippers until 1949. By then, the number of Swedish speakers had declined and the church was sold to the Masons. Christine was called "Mama Johnson" because of her kindness to all who met her, especially the new Swedish immigrants.

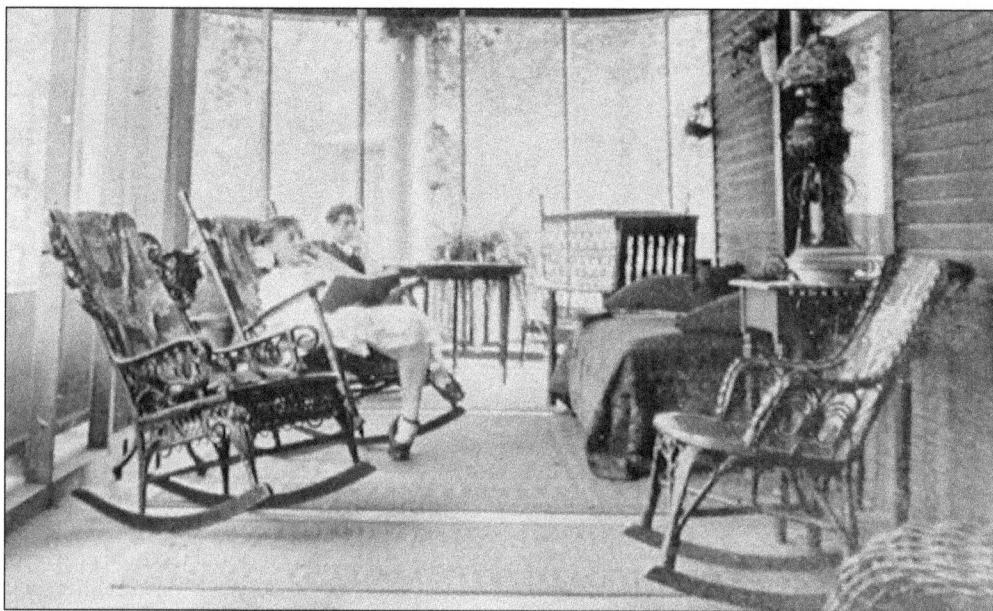

Relaxing on their screened porch at 4312 Central Ave. are Dorothy Chapman (left) and her mother Bessie (Bailey) Chapman. Bessie's husband, Charles A. Chapman, was a construction engineer who was president of the village from 1915 to 1921. This home later burned and was demolished.

Fourth of July in 1921 is celebrated in the backyard of the Cropp home at 4381 Central Ave. (This home still stood in 2001.) Independence Day meant parades and sporting events in Western Springs. Enjoying a picnic lunch are the Cropps and their neighbors, from left to right, Carl Cropp, Ellen Williams, Mr. Fox, Leonard H. Vaughan, Edith Williams, Lydia J. (Terrell) Williams, and Kate Williams.

Children enjoy the wading pool at the Council Home (later burned and demolished) on the southeast corner of Oak Street and Lawn Avenue. Evangelist John Alexander Dowie originally built this building sometime before 1907. From 1908 to c. 1922, the National Council of Jewish Women owned and operated this building as a fresh-air camp for underprivileged children and their mothers from Chicago.

An even dozen of little children enjoy a birthday party at the home of Elmore C. Patterson at 4344 Grand Ave. This photo was taken about 1911 when large hair bows were in fashion. Pictured, from left to right, the partygoers are Constance McClure, Lucy Gale, Ruth Rose, Elmore Hammesfahr, Dorothy Gale, unidentified, Helen Gollan, four unidentified, and Martha Patterson in the baby stroller.

In 1913, a group of schoolchildren from Western Springs paddle several boats on the millpond by the Graue Mill in Oak Brook. Although Salt Creek does not flow through Western Springs, it was a popular spot for outings since it was a larger stream than Flag Creek. Salt Creek is so named because, according to legend, a wagon of salt dumped over in it in the 1800s. Flag Creek gets its name from the many reeds (also known as flags) that grew along its banks.

Another group of schoolchildren enjoys an outing in Salt Creek in 1914. The Forest Preserve of Cook County was established in 1914, and included the portion of Salt Creek that flows within this county. Salt Creek is about 50 miles long and flows through 30 communities. Downstream of Western Springs, the creek flows northward for a short distance—one of the few streams in Illinois to do so.

In 1912, despite long white dresses, women (married vs. single) played baseball as part of the July Fourth activities. The single women beat the married women that year 16 to 8. Other athletic events that year include egg-on-a-spoon and potato-on-a-spoon races. A cornet band supplied the musical entertainment.

At a men's ballgame in 1914, nine young women provided the refreshment in the form of homemade lemonade. The women, from left to right, are Elizabeth Titsworth Mitchell, Helen Murphy McKay, Lucille Sanders, Rosetta Hoag Dearborn, Pearl Winternitz Morris, Rebecca Harland Morgan, Eleanor Blount Ford, unidentified, and Alice Bush.

Dressed in the height of fashion, a group of young people prepare for a tennis match on the lawn in front of the Henthorne house at 4471 Lawn Ave. (In 2001, this home was used as an office.) Tennis was introduced to the United States in 1874. It was apparently a descendant of an English game called court tennis. The first championship match at Wimbledon, England, was held in 1877. The first national women's tennis championships were held in the U.S. in 1887 at a time when women, despite their confining clothes, were beginning to play sports. A number of families in Western Springs had grass courts on their property, including the Henthornes at 4471 Lawn Ave., the Winternitzes at 1206 Walnut St., and the Vaughans at 1111 Walnut St. These homes still stood in 2001. Pictured, from left to right, are Ellen Williams, three unidentified, Florence Henthorne, and two more unidentified.

Pearl Winternitz (left) and Charlotte Titsworth compare racquets on the tennis court behind the Winternitz home at 1206 Walnut St. in 1914. The Winternitz home was known to many people in the village and beyond because of the small zoo in its backyard. Residents of the zoo included monkeys, deer, ponies, ducks, chickens, and fish. (This home still stood in 2001.)

Ethel Hanneman (born c. 1902) prepares to volley on the front lawn of the Winternitz home. The home's owner, Samuel L. Winternitz, a Jewish immigrant from Czechoslovakia, was a successful auctioneer who loved animals. The length of Ethel's skirt, compared to other women's tennis costumes, indicates that this photo must have been taken in the 1920s.

Decked out in stylish tennis togs, Edwin Henthorne is ready for a game of lawn tennis at his home at 4471 Lawn Ave. in the 1890s. (In 2001, this house was used as an office building.) This photo was originally taken with a glass negative, probably with a Vive Camera manufactured in Western Springs. Glass negatives were popular from about 1850 to the 1880s when gelatin-based flexible film was introduced.

Football was popular with the young men in the village. This unidentified young man wears a lace-up body suit with protective padding. The first football game was played in New Jersey in 1869 between Rutgers and Princeton universities. There were 25 men on each side. The players yelled at opposing team members to unnerve them. Later, in order to save the strength of the players, spectators did the yelling.

These young lads are part of Boy Scout Troop #1, the first in Western Springs, and one of the earliest in the country. A Chicago publisher named William Boyce founded the Boy Scouts of America in 1910 and patterned it after similar organizations in Canada and Great Britain. The scouting organization aimed to train boys, build character, and promote physical development through a program stressing work, outdoor play, and community duty. The troops were divided into three levels: tenderfoots, second-class scouts, and first-class scouts. Pictured in this 1912 photo, from left to right, are the following: (front row) Kenneth Newcomer, Milton Keil, William Neiman, William Ford, Adolph Winternitz, and Alfred Stocker; (back row) Elliot Quinby, Emil Arbeen, Emmett Gustafson, Fred Edwards, Newell Ford, Hiram Parks Jr., and Ralph McClelland. The scoutmasters (not shown) that year were Horace Denton and Harold Joy.

The year 1910 also marked the founding of the Campfire Girls organization in the U.S. This organization was similar to the Boy Scouts, but was based "on the supposition that the center of feminine activities is and should be, the home, where the fire must always be kept burning, and that in order to increase the efficiency of the keeper of that fire she must 'seek beauty, give service, pursue knowledge, hold on to health, glorify work and be happy.' " The girls went on hiking trips, marched in local parades, and ventured into the poorer neighborhoods of Chicago with suitcases of clothes that they distributed to the needy. The three ranks in the Camp Fire girls were: wood gatherer, fire maker, and torchbearer. Pictured, from left to right, are unidentified, unidentified, Frances Omlag, Dorothy Breed, Lucy Gale, and the rest are unidentified.

In 1908, the Western Springs Athletic Association members posed for this photo that may have been taken in Chicago. Western Springs teams often played the teams from other communities along the "Q"—the Chicago, Burlington, and Quincy Railroad. Team members, from left to right, are the following: (front row) Luther Fernon, John E. Williams, ? Stevens (mascot), Emory Patterson, and unidentified; (back row) unidentified, Malcolm Hart, unidentified, unidentified, and Allen Craig.

On a spring day in 1920, kids play in the slough near Vaughan's Seed Company's greenhouses. The greenhouses were located about where Reid Street was in 2001. The slough was part of the marshy area along Flag Creek. In dry weather, the marsh dried up and sometimes caught fire and smoldered underground. Children, from left to right, are Grace Earl, Carma Rohedder, Charles Vaughan, Edna Gustafson, Walter Burr, Robert Vaughan, and Leslie Nelson.

58

On Tuesday afternoon, June 15, 1897, an unidentified woman (left) and Florence Henthorne, a piano teacher, sat on the banks of Salt Creek and probably never thought that their photo would be enjoyed by people in the 21st century in this book. Salt Creek was much cleaner at that date; people used to catch fish weighing up to 10 pounds there.

More adventurous than young women in long skirts, these six young men perched precariously above the waters of Salt Creek. In the 1920s, the Forest Preserve built a dam just west of Wolf Road to create a swimming hole for kids. The dam was removed in 1932 when the stream became polluted by communities upstream.

July 4, 1895, fell on a Thursday and these picnickers took advantage of the day off to picnic in the woods near Salt Creek. A 1918 Forest Preserve publication describes the Salt Creek area this way: "Great forests of oaks and maples and hickory and elm, inhabited by every known specie of animal and bird life—those extinct are being revived—and capped with a variety of flowers and fauna worthy of a horticulturist's dream, are found here." The reference to the horticulturist may refer to John C. Vaughan, the founder of the seed company in Western Springs. Vaughan was one of the citizen members of the plan committee that founded the Cook County Forest Preserve. The Forest Preserve initially planned to turn the forest preserve into a series of manicured parks, but later opted to leave the natural beauty of this area. Pictured, from left to right, are Charles H. "Daddy" Rowe, Ella E. Rowe, unidentified, unidentified, Houston C. Adcock, three unidentified, Jessie Rowe, and unidentified.

60

Five

PORTRAITS OF
OUR PAST

The history of a place is, after all, the history of the people who lived there. The people who posed for the photos on these pages were all aware that someone was taking their photo. Some look as though they knew at the time that their photo would become part of history. Others seem rooted in the moment and appear to be aware only of themselves and the camera.

A professional photographer took many of the more formal portraits in a studio. Often there is a clear reason for the portrait—a wedding, the birth of a child, or a birthday.

There were probably more amateur photographers in Western Springs in the 1800s than in most suburban communities because of the Vive Camera Company. Some of the photos in this book were taken with Vive cameras that used glass-plate negatives. The Vive Camera Co. closed its doors several years after Kodak introduced the Brownie box camera. This camera used flexible film which amateur photographers could remove and send out for processing. This system of photography formed the basis of most 20th-century photography. In the last decade of that century, digital cameras became increasingly popular. These cameras reduced images to tiny dots and stored this information on small magnetic strips. Most of the photos in this book were originally produced on glass-plate negatives or on flexible film. The prints of these photos were rephotographed with a digital camera in order to be reproduced for this book.

In the summer of 1898, the Arbeen family poses for a photo near Salt Creek. Claes Otto Arbeen and his wife Charlotte (Sand) Arbeen were Swedish immigrants in their early thirties who immigrated to the Midwest in the early 1880s with their three children. After a few years in Chicago, they settled in Western Springs in 1886 to join the other Swedes in the village and continued adding to their family. (One more was added after this photo was taken.) Arbeen originally worked as a cobbler, then worked at the Chicago Casket Company for 47 years. The Arbeens, from left to right, are as follows: (front row) Hulda, Charlotte, Victor, Claes, and Tillie; (back row) Susan, Charles, Ida, and Ruth. Emil (not shown) was born later in 1898. The Arbeens lived first at 4636 Woodland Ave. and later at 4641 Woodland Ave. (These homes were later demolished.)

One of the earliest groups of settlers in the village in the 1870s and 1880s was the Quakers. They built their picturesque wooden church on the southwest corner of Woodland Avenue and Walnut Street. Quakers Sarah (Atwater) Kelsey and her husband Asa Kelsey moved to Western Springs in 1875. Sarah's parents were well-known Quaker ministers in New York State. Sarah raised five children here and was a minister in the Western Springs Quaker church. She also helped found the Village Sewing Society that was open to any woman in the village. Sarah was a member of the Women's Christian Temperance Union, an organization that opposed the consumption of alcohol. It was probably the influence of the Quakers that made Western Springs a "dry" community for more than 100 years. Asa Kelsey, also a Quaker, was a dealer in coffee and spices.

Walter Dwight Dana (five months old here) was born in Kansas in 1886, but spent much of his youth in Western Springs. His family moved here in 1891. In 1898, his father caught "gold fever," and spent three years hunting for gold in the Klondike area of Alaska while his wife and family stayed here. The family donated this baby dress to the Western Springs Historical Society Museum.

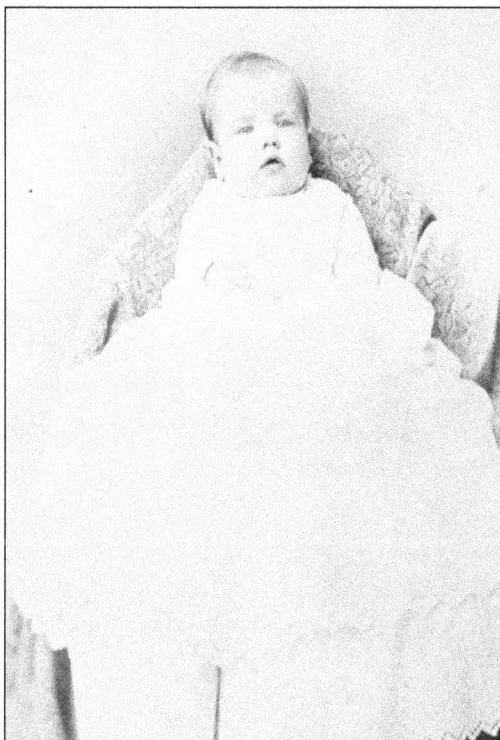

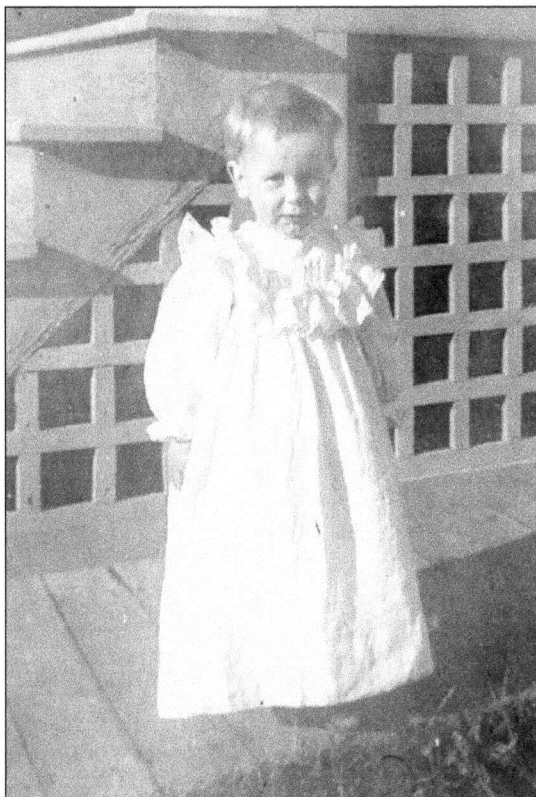

This is how little boys were dressed in the late 1700s and 1800s. The loose garment was called a *frock*. Harold Lane's hair is short, but some boys had long hair. By school age, boys wore knickers (knee pants) and long socks. Older boys graduated to long pants. This photo was taken *c.* 1900.

A c. 1900 photo shows two children photographed with a Vive Camera. Both are children of Swedish immigrants living in the village: Edwin Pearson and Hilma Ekdahl. Ekdahl's father was a shoemaker in Western Springs. Pearson's father worked at Vaughan's Seed Company, and repaired bicycles.

On the day of her eighth grade graduation (c. 1909), Elsie Peterson posed for this photo in a white dress trimmed with lace. A large white bow holds back her hair. Elsie's family donated this dress to the Western Springs Historical Society Museum. Elsie became a caterer when she grew up. She never married.

The Ekdahl family posed for this photo about 1905. Pictured, from left to right, are Augusta Ekdahl, August Ekdahl, and their son Carl Ekdahl. Immigrants from Sweden, the Ekdahl family was fairly prosperous. In 1890, August built a substantial two-story frame building on Hillgrove Avenue. This building housed his store and the post office in its early years. Villagers had to come to the post office to pick up mail. Augusta was well known in the village because she baked excellent angel food cakes. Carl was born in Western Springs in 1899.

One of the most talented women in the village, Mary Gladys (Tredwell) Cattell, settled in Western Springs with her new husband Jonas Herbert Cattell in 1914. She raised four children (here she holds Mary, her first child), and in 1929, she founded the Theatre of Western Springs, an organization that was still active in 2001.

Axel and Louise (Johnson) Carlson married in 1888 and sat for this formal portrait. They first lived in Hinsdale and did not move to Western Springs until sometime later. They left few records of their lives here other than this photograph. It is difficult to research someone with such a common name as Axel Carlson.

In contrast, we know a lot about this couple—Albert and Anna (Lundquist) Erickson—who were married on June 26, 1901. Their adopted son Waldo Erickson married Maude Lane who eventually became the first archivist of the Western Springs Historical Society. Albert Erickson worked for the Vaughan's Seed Company for 63 years.

The Baldwin family moved to Western Springs in 1909, although this photo was taken more than a decade earlier (c. 1895) when the family lived in Chicago. The Baldwins were originally from New York State. Pictured, from left to right, are Estella Maybell (Bushnell) Baldwin, Gertrude Baldwin, Charlotte Baldwin, and Charles Harvey Baldwin. They lived in a large house on the southeast corner of Chestnut Street and Central Avenue. The home burned in 1917.

Albert married Frieda Mathilda Eckstrand on June 26, 1909. Albert was a Norwegian immigrant who built many homes in Western Springs. Frieda was from Sweden. They probably met in Western Springs when Frieda came to stay with "Mama Johnson" who was a friend of her mother's.

Charles Gustafson was another successful builder/contractor in Western Springs. He left his native Sweden in 1887 and settled in the village sometime after that. He married Frieda Holstrom (also spelled Hilstrom) in 1902. Frieda and her family had been living in Western Springs since 1890. Gustafson built numerous homes in the village, but perhaps his most important work was the building of the Swedish Methodist Church at 1215 Chestnut St. in 1893. (That building was still standing in 2001.) In 1890, Illinois' Swedish population numbered 128,897, or about 10 percent of the immigrants living in Illinois. Germans, more numerous by far, made up 40 percent of Illinois' foreign-born residents. It is unclear why a Swedish enclave developed in Western Springs. Some of the Swedish residents worked for Vaughan's Seed Company, so perhaps this was the reason. The Swedish Methodist Church was the only church in the village that conducted services in a foreign language.

Sober and serious looking, John Holden served as the Western Springs village marshal from 1900 to 1912, when he moved to California. Western Springs did not have a police department until 1925. Before that, the village marshal was responsible for keeping the peace and enforcing the laws.

Another person who appeared devoid of humor was John A. Comstock. He appears on a postcard when he was running for the office of village tax collector. Comstock was devoted to his work. He served as a village trustee from 1909 to 1915 and never missed a meeting. He lived near the intersection of Hampton Avenue and Walnut Street where he had a large strawberry patch.

One of the most familiar faces to villagers in the late 1800s and early 1900s was "Daddy" Rowe. Clarence H. Rowe served as the Western Springs marshal from 1895 to 1897, and then again from about 1914 to about 1920. "Daddy" was a common appellation for a local marshal. A retired man often filled this position. He dealt with hoboes, rabid dogs, and had no patience for strangers he didn't like the looks of. The *Western Springs Times* often contained mentions of Rowe's actions. In 1914, he "convinced a band of gypsies that the groves on South East Boulevard [the southern portion of Wolf Road] were neither safe nor convenient places for them to erect their tents." In that same year, the paper reported that Rowe had jailed a stranger whose only offense was a "dippy" appearance. Rowe, however, was popular with the village children, and he frequently led the parade on the Fourth of July.

Marjorie Hoffman settled in Western Springs in 1892. She lived with her parents Mr. and Mrs. George Hoffman, and her three brothers Paul, James, and Hallech. They lived at 4142 Grove Ave. (This house still existed in 2001.) The family moved to California in 1908. Her brother Paul later became the chairman of the board of the Studebaker Corporation, and then president of the Ford Foundation.

Standing in her backyard vegetable garden on a sunny day with a friend (unidentified), is Mildred (Wakefield) Cornell. Cornell and her husband H.L. Cornell had five children, three of whom died before the age of seven. Her two remaining sons both served in World War I. The Cornells lived at 1320 Chestnut St. (This home was later demolished.)

Ethel Frances Banker posed for a formal portrait c. 1910 with her hair done up in the stylish pompadour style. Many women who wore this hair style used sausage-shaped hair pieces (popularly called "rats") to provide the desired shape. Ethel was born in 1889. Her father, William H. Banker, owned a grocery and meat market in the village in the 1890s and first decade of the 20th century.

Frances A. Blount is seen here in a photo c. 1900. Frances and her husband, Sylvester Pierce Blount, raised two daughters and a son. Sylvester was the president of the village in 1896. Frances was active in church and community work.

Sabina (Ruth) Arnold sat for her photo in 1910 when she was 63. She was born in Long Grove, Illinois, in 1847 and married Civil War veteran Daniel Allen Arnold in 1866. They raised three daughters and moved to Chicago. Sabina and her husband moved to the village in 1899 when they were in their fifties to be close to their daughter. The Arnolds also wanted a home with room for a garden. They purchased one of the best-known older homes in the village—at 4364 Grand Ave. The Arnold's granddaughter, Ruth Rose, recalled that her grandfather was "a compulsive gardener, rising at sunrise and allowing just time to catch the morning train … returning on the 5:15, he gardened until dark and sometimes after…" His photo appears in chapters 1 and 5. Daniel died in 1911. Sabina was the oldest voter in Western Springs in the 1940 election. She died in 1941 at the age of 93. This home still stood in 2001.

Dorothy Chapman was a schoolteacher who taught at the Ogden Avenue School in La Grange in the 1920s. Her father, Charles A. Chapman, was the village president from 1915 to 1921. Dorothy and her family lived in a large home at 4312 Central Ave. This home burned and was demolished sometime after 1930.

This daring young woman (Mary Bowers) in her riding attire was photographed c. 1918 as she stood on the northwest corner of Woodland and Hillgrove avenues. (Women did not commonly wear pants at that time.) The 4368 Grand Ave. home is on the right. This home was later demolished.

The first historian of Western Springs was Albert William Macy who arrived in Western Springs in 1887. When he moved to the village, there were 400 to 500 people. There were no sewers, electric lights, paved streets, or water system, and the sidewalks were made of wooden planks. Macy served on the school board, was a village trustee from 1904 to 1909, and served as village clerk from 1910 to 1916. For this latter position, he received $25 per month. Macy was born in Indiana in 1878. He was also a freelance writer and syndicated columnist whose column "Curious Bits of History" appeared in more than 20 newspapers in the early 1900s. His greatest contribution to the history of the village was a scrapbook of newspaper clippings that he kept over the years. He donated this to the village and it was given to the Western Springs Historical Society when it was formed.

Laura (Wellman) Dana posed for this photo on March 2, 1944, when she was 85 years old. Born in Iowa in 1859, she married Luther Greene Dana in 1882, farmed with him in Iowa and Kansas, and raised three children. When Laura and her family moved to Western Springs in 1891, they brought their cow "Daisy" with them. Luther caught "gold fever" in 1898 and spent three years in Alaska during the Klondike Gold Rush. Laura died in 1959 at the age of 100.

Mary Niemann was a musician who lived in Western Springs in the late 1930s. She was a well-known pianist who had appeared with the Chicago Symphony Orchestra. Mary taught piano and ran the Niemann School of Music from her home at 1206 Walnut St. (This home still stood in 2001.) She was also the director of the choir at the Congregational Church.

Six

"CALLING ALL CARS"

A ccidents happen. When they happened in Western Springs, residents and village employees have always pitched in to help.

When fires occurred in the 1800s, citizens formed impromptu bucket brigades to fight fires. Time brought gradual improvements such as a hose cart that was hauled behind a car, a truck with ladders, and a snorkel truck. One of the proudest moments in the history of the Fire Department came when they placed first in a national firefighters' contest in 1937. One of the more visible fires occurred in 1991 when the roof of the village's historic water tower was struck by lightning and caught fire.

In the 1800s and early 1900s, a village marshal maintained law and order by throwing any suspicious-looking strangers into the "calaboose" (jail) for the night. The police department was organized in 1925. Its first patrol officers used telephones to communicate with the headquarters in the water tower. When headquarters wanted the officers to phone in, they turned on a light at the top of the water tower. The department was organized during Prohibition, so some of the early actions by the police involved people using or manufacturing alcohol.

There were three spectacular train accidents between 1909 and 1915. In each case, the village residents ran to assist the victims.

As aviation became more popular, there were at least six plane wrecks in Western Springs. By this time, there were established emergency services in the village, but residents still contributed by serving coffee to emergency personnel.

The residents of this home at 4241 Franklin Ave. must have been more than a little surprised and shaken up to find that an airplane had landed in their front yard on March 31, 1931. Ralph Wilson of La Grange piloted the plane. He took off from the Chicago Municipal Airport (later renamed Midway Airport). Wilson apparently lost control of the plane at about 1,500 feet and fell to the ground. He eventually recovered from his injuries.

On a freezing night in February 1917, a fire broke out in a clothes chute in the home of the Charles H. Baldwin family at the southwest corner of Central Avenue and Chestnut Street. The local paper described it as "the most disastrous fire that has happened in Western Springs in some time. The equipment of the fire department proved hopelessly inadequate to save the building, but the firemen did heroic work in preventing the flames from spreading."

Flames consumed one of the last vestiges of farming in Western Springs on June 3, 1968— the old Dierks' barn at 5160 Willow Springs Rd. Dietrich Dierks and his family farmed this area in the late 1800s and early 1900s. His children, Ernest and Caroline, sold the farm to the Springdale Development Company. (See chapter 1 for more information.)

Just 10 years before this book was written, one of the most memorable fires in the village's history occurred. On August 30, 1991, about 1 a.m., lightning apparently struck the roof of the 1892 water tower, just one month after the Western Springs Historical Society had begun plans to celebrate the tower's centennial. The fire smoldered under the roof for hours. Neighbors smelled smoke and called the fire department, but the fire did not break through the roof until almost 5 a.m. when early commuters reported seeing 30-foot-high flames shooting up from the roof. The empty 113,000-gallon water tank under the roof hampered firefighters' efforts to extinguish the flames. Firefighters used tarps to protect the irreplaceable items in the collection of the Historical Society's Museum on the first and second floors. After two years of repair and restoration, the museum reopened.

On December 18, 1909, at about 4 a.m., a long-distance express passenger train, the *Oriental Limited*, was speeding along the tracks west of Western Springs. The train was more than seven hours behind schedule and was speeding to make up for the delay. One of the cars hit a broken rail and the train derailed. Several hundred feet of track were torn up as the train left the track and slid along the ground. It finally stopped upside down in a ditch 20 feet below the tracks about where the Spring Rock Park was in 2001. Twenty people were injured, but all survived. Rescue workers banged on the doors of nearby homes and asked for donations of sheets that could be used as emergency bandages. Citizens of Hinsdale and Western Springs helped care for the victims until they could be transported to local hospitals.

Just three years after the *Oriental Limited* wreck, on a foggy Sunday morning of July 20, 1912, a Transcontinental Mail train, traveling at 60 or 70 miles an hour, hit the *Overland Limited* passenger train east of Wolf Road. Thirteen people were killed and more than 20 were injured. The women of Western Springs ran to the aid of the victims with sheets, bandages, and blankets.

Three years after *that* wreck, another train wreck occurred on September 20, 1915, at almost the same spot. This time, a westbound long-distance express passenger train ran into a freight train. Again, Western Springs residents helped the injured until emergency crews were able to reach the scene.

The village's first firehouse (*c.* 1922) was a one-room building that sat on the north side of Walnut Street between Lawn and Grand avenues, just north of the water tower. In 1923, it was moved to the west side of Wolf Road, and later moved to the east side where it was added on to (see below), and continued to be used for storage for decades.

Volunteer firefighters are seen here in the 1920s practicing with hose and ladder in front of the once-handsome original firehouse building. The men, from left to right, are Carl Bollnow, Harold Anderson, Roy Karstens, Waldo Erickson, three unidentified, and Cyril Dean.

Undoubtedly the proudest day in the history of the Western Springs Fire Department was September 6, 1937. The all-volunteer firefighters competed with other volunteer teams from all over the country at Chicago's Soldier Field in the first National Firefighters' tournament. The Western Springs group, led by Chief Waldo Erickson, won first prize in the contest to rescue a victim from a second-story window with a ladder and ropes. Their skill in other events such as wall climbing, ladder raising, and laying 300 feet of hose earned them the all-around first prize of $500. Other events at the contest included water fights, fire alarm turnouts, life net drills, sliding down ropes, and salvage drills. From left to right are Albert Lundin, Cutler Wolf, Harvey Ogren, Arthur Winkelman, Ernest Johnson, Walter Mayer, George Schreder, Waldo Erickson, George Winkelman, John Ogren, Lester Warner, Walfrid Wohlstrom, and Roy Karstens.

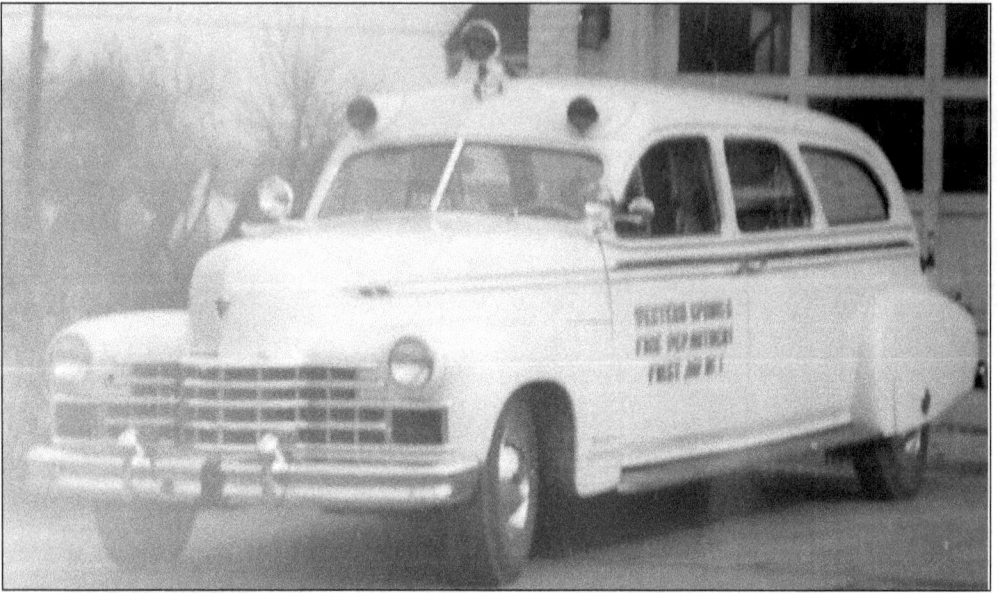

This white Cadillac ambulance made its debut in Western Springs on May 8, 1948. The vehicle included two stretchers in back and a two-way radio. Half of the cost for the ambulance came from funds left over from the World War II Civil Defense Fund, and the remainder was raised by scrap drives and donations. In 1948, the village charged $12 for a trip of up to 3 miles. This vehicle served the department for more than 20 years.

In 1960, this small vehicle began to be used by the dog warden to round up stray dogs, other pets, and wild animals such as raccoons. Occasionally, more exotic pets such as iguanas would escape and lead to calls to the police department from startled residents who reported "giant lizards" in their backyards.

The village's first fire truck was sorely needed when it was acquired in 1923. (In prior years, the volunteers jumped into a car or truck and hauled a hose cart behind them to the fire.) This truck was used for 30 years. The truck was purchased with money raised at the 1923 firemen's festival, and was referred to as "the pride of the village." In 1924, the Fire Department's motto was "protection, public welfare, and village improvements."

National Fire Prevention Week ran from Oct. 5th to 11th in 1969 when this photo was taken. The photographer stood on the roof of Lyons Township High School's South Campus to snap the Western Springs Fire Department's vehicles and firefighters. In the years before 911 emergency numbers and caller identification, residents who called to report a fire had to dial 246 and four more digits, and provide information about the location of the fire or emergency.

The members of the Western Springs Police Department pose for a photo c. 1951. Western Springs did not have a police department until 1925. Before that, beginning in 1885, there was a village marshal and perhaps a deputy or two. (Two of the marshals appear in chapter 5.) For many years, the police department and the court, along with other village offices, were housed on the first and second floors of the 1892 water tower. The police department was formed during Prohibition, and there were numerous stories in the local newspaper about the police raiding illegal stills in the village. In the years before two-way radios, a light on top of the old water tower would be used to alert police who would then find a public phone and call to find out what the problem was. The policemen, from left to right, are Howard Smurz, Robert ?, Chief Clarence J. Buehl, Paul Behnke, Charles Peterson, unidentified, Guy O'Haver, Herbert May, and George Schreder.

Seven

IN WAR AND IN PEACE

World Wars I and II called for participation from Western Springs residents and affected their day-to-day lives more than any wars before or since. While young men (and a small number of young women) joined the armed forces and left the village to take part in or support armed conflicts, the men, women, and children on the home front all helped "do their bit" to help the war effort.

During World War I, grade school children in Western Springs knitted tiny squares of wool yarn which women then stitched into blankets. High school boys practiced military-style marching, and high school girls rolled cotton cloth into bandages. Men and women planted "victory gardens" in yards and empty lots to increase the food supply. Housewives struggled to create balanced meals in spite of shortages or rationing that limited such staples as meat, cooking oil, wheat flour, and sugar. History was made during World War I when Western Springer Charlotte Titsworth served as one of only 305 women marines in that war.

Everyone participated in conserving and recycling items made of paper, metal, or rubber. The issues of the *Western Springs Times* newspapers during World War I are all missing—probably the result of scrap drives.

The patriotic activities most frequently photographed were the July Fourth parades, games, and picnics. Fifteen hundred people attended the Independence Day celebration in 1926 that marked the 150th anniversary of the signing of the Declaration of Independence and also the 40th anniversary of the village.

Standing proudly on his truck decorated for a Fourth of July parade sometime in the 1920s or 1930s, is Ed Perrott, a general contractor who specialized in cement work. Residents decorated cars, trucks, horse wagons, and even doll carriages for the big parade that was held the morning of the Fourth. Pictured, from left to right, are George Perrott, Edna Perrott, Louise Perrott, Minnie Perrott, Ed Perrott, and Mrs. Perrott.

Lucy Ellen Blair, all decked out in a patriotic dress, poses for a photo c. 1906. Lucy was the oldest of five children. Her family moved to Western Springs in 1903. Lucy's father was a commercial artist. Lucy had her own business as a hairdresser in the 1920s, 30s, and 40s.

Standing straight and tall is Civil War veteran Daniel Allen Arnold. Arnold wears the uniform of the Civil War veterans' organization—the Grand Army of the Republic. The GAR founded soldiers' homes and was active in relief work and pension legislation. Wives of veterans formed a group called the Women's Relief Corps.

The only Western Springs resident to die in action overseas during World War I was Henry G. Maxted. He was born in 1885 in Canada, and his family moved to Western Springs in 1888. Maxted worked his way through college and later worked in Boston for the Massachusetts Society for the Prevention of Cruelty to Children. He joined the National Guard and was sent to France in 1917. He died in action in April 1918.

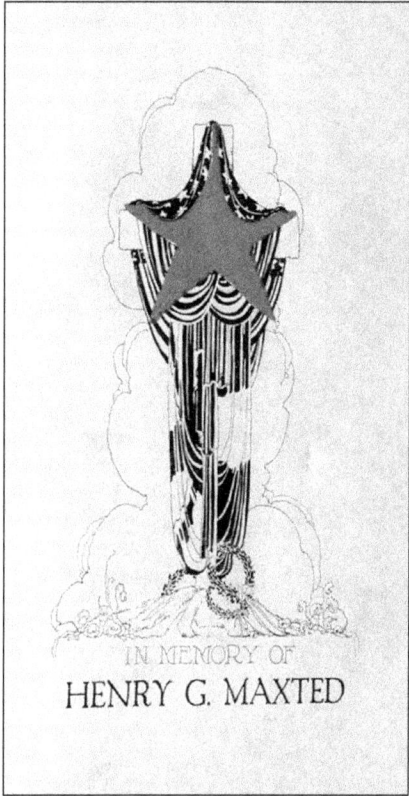

IN MEMORY OF

HENRY G. MAXTED

Henry G. (Harry) Maxted was the oldest of eight children in the Maxted family. The family lived at 619 47th St. (The house still stood in 2001.) The Maxteds had a small dairy, and Harry and his brothers and sisters sometimes helped deliver milk on their way to the Grand Avenue School.

Donald Cornell served in the United States Air Force in World War I. His brother Arthur served in the infantry. The United States entered the war on April 6, 1917. Fortunately for the Cornell family, both young men returned safely. Their mother had watched her first three children die in their childhood. Her photo appears in Chapter 5.

Private Emil F. Arbeen began his service with the 123rd H.F. Artillery at Camp Logan in Houston, Texas, on October 15, 1917. Arbeen was born and raised in Western Springs. A photo of his family appears in Chapter 5. Arbeen is shown with his Boy Scout troop in Chapter 4. He was the youngest of 10 children.

Proudly wearing her World War I Marine Corps uniform is 20-year-old Charlotte Titsworth of Western Springs. Titsworth was one of only 305 women who served in the Marines during the First World War. This did not surprise people who knew her. In high school in 1914, she took a class in woodshop (unheard of at that time) and made a bookcase. The female Marines all served in non-combat positions. Titsworth did clerical work in Washington in order to "free a man to fight." The Marines ordered all the women to leave the Corps in 1919 when the war was over. Titsworth later worked for the Department of Agriculture, and the Department of Veterans Affairs (later known as the Veterans Administration). When she retired at age 70 in 1968, she was one of the highest-ranking women in the VA. She was considered one of the pioneers who paved the way for future women to work in the armed forces. Charlotte (Titsworth) Austin died in 1995 at the age of 97.

Second Lieutenant William Samuel Quinby was the first young man from Western Springs to serve in Europe. He wrote letters to his parents describing his feelings about being in a war zone with bomb shelters and gas masks, and the sensation that each moment might be his last. Quinby was the first World War I soldier to be sent home, and was in Western Springs when the war ended. He later reenlisted and served in China.

In 1917, many of the remaining men in Western Springs formed a Home Guard unit. Pictured, from left to right, are the following: (front row) E. Stocker, ? Hanneman, ? Hamilton, W. Kennedy, H. Cattell, R. McClelland, ? Brundage, W. Gollan, F. Horner, F. Titsworth, E. Murphy, and D. Kennedy; (back row) A. Stocker, P. Gladden, G. Morgan, W.C. Anderson, H. Joy, G. Newcomb, C. White, H. Lane, E.C. Patterson, H. Keil, ? Bodman, W.D. Dana, ? Applegate, and ? Merrick.

Many of the women in the village volunteered for the local Red Cross. Women helped the war effort by preparing meals that conserved the country's food resources. At first, Tuesdays were declared "meatless days," and Wednesdays were "wheatless days." Later there were two meatless days and two wheatless days each week, in additions to gasless Sundays, lightless nights, and porkless days. Items such as sugar were rationed, but women who canned their own fruit were allowed extra allotments. Schoolchildren knitted one-inch-squares of wool which women sewed into blankets. "Victory gardens" were everywhere as people grew their own vegetables. At Lyons Township High School, boys practiced military marching and girls rolled bandages. LT students also voted to postpone buying their class sweaters in order to conserve wool. Younger children put on skits to earn extra coins for the war effort. Everyone asked each other, "Are you doing your bit [to help the war effort]?"

Children march along the CB&Q tracks in the Fourth of July Parade in 1918. During the war years, there was an increase in patriotic activities. After the parade, there were numerous contests for the children and adults. The games included climbing a greased pole with a dollar on top, a ladies' bean bag throwing contest, a sack race, a potato-on-a-spoon race, and a pie-eating contest.

The celebration on July 4, 1926, was extra special. This date marked the 150th anniversary of the signing of the Declaration of Independence. Western Springs was also 40 years old. An estimated 1,500 people watched the parade that year. Present here, from left to right, are George Hill, Walter Hartstein, John Edwards, Horrace Collom, and Russell J. James.

Rationing occurred again during World War II. Rationed items included sugar, coffee, butter, meat, cheese, flour, fish, canned goods, tires, and shoes. Here, c. 1942, the Western Springs Rationing Board makes decisions about the distribution of gasoline ration books to residents. Pictured, from left to right, are two unidentified, John Hooper, two more unidentified, and probably Dorothy Hubner (ration board secretary).

On a chilly autumn day—October 11, 1942—70 Western Springs men and women gathered to take part in a "super-scrap salvage campaign." They collected 48 tons of metal and 26 tons of paper that were hauled away in 11 trucks donated by local businesses. The house in the background at 4392 Woodland Ave. has been demolished.

Scrap drives occurred repeatedly during the war. During the summer of 1942, Western Springers contributed 2,600 pounds of tin cans. Old stoves and washtubs were among the items this day. The 4392 Woodland Ave. house (later demolished) is in the background. In addition to scrap drives, people also donated blood. Women's groups contributed to the war effort by organizing "sewing bees" at which they sewed uniforms. Rationing and doing without was not always easy. One item in the local paper read: "We sure are beginning to feel the pinch of gasoline rationing around home. We can't get in our car and drive off some place any time we want to, like we used to do. Tires are getting thin and with so many mechanics working in war plants, we have to leave a car in the garage much longer now when some repairs are needed."

Eight

WE GATHER TOGETHER

The oldest churches in Western Springs—the Quaker Meeting House and the Swedish Methodist Church—were both built in the 1800s, and both congregations were dissolved by the mid-1900s. The Quaker Meeting House, at the southwest corner of Woodland Avenue and Walnut Street was sold to the Episcopal Church, which replaced it with a brick church. The Swedish Methodist Church at 1215 Chestnut St. was sold to the Masons who still owned it in 2001.

The best-known person to serve in a Western Springs church was Billy Graham. In 1943, he became the pastor of the Village (Baptist) Church and began radio broadcasts of a religious program from the church basement. He later became a world-famous evangelist.

Probably the most architecturally significant church is the First Congregational Church of Western Springs—designed by Prairie School architect G. Grant Elmslie. St. John of the Cross Church is the only church that has a school, and the Episcopal congregation has the distinction of being the only one that formerly held services in the water tower.

In 1950, just before breaking ground for their new church, the members of the First United Methodist Church posed for a photo. Pictured, from left to right, are the following: (front row) two unidentified, Joan Lindahl, three unidentified, and Billy Bower; (second row) unidentified, Virginia Lindahl, Alice Eilenfeldt, unidentified, Mary Bower holding Robert Bower, and Rev. Lloyd M. Bower; (third row) unidentified, Arthur Eilenfeldt, Louise Sutton, John Blang, Dorothy Blang, Joe Lindahl, Mabel Lindahl, and four unidentified; (back row) six unidentified, Russell Larson, and three unidentified.

The most famous of the people associated with churches in Western Springs was the Rev. Billy Graham. In 1943, Billy Graham, newly graduated from Wheaton College, was invited to become the new pastor at the Village (Baptist) Church in Western Springs. Graham began broadcasting his *Songs in the Night* radio program on January 2, 1944. The members of the church raised the $85 per week that was necessary to air the program. Each program began with the words, "Coming to you from the friendly church in the pleasant community of Western Springs." Graham continued the program, but left the church after the radio program had been running for several months. The program's soloist was George Beverly Shea and the organist was Donald Husted. Shown in this photo, from left to right, are Henry Paynter, Mrs. Burton W. Rhoads, Clifford White, Billy Graham, Charles Rhoads, Mrs. Charles Rhoads, Burton W. Rhoads, Mrs. William Grabow, and William Grabow.

The Village (Baptist) Church building (4475 Wolf Rd.) was begun in 1937. The church was built in stages. In 1937, the church basement was built. It was from here that Billy Graham broadcast his radio program. The basement served as the church until the first floor was built in 1949. In 1957, and educational wing was added on. This photo shows the church in 1945.

On December 9, 2001, the members of the Village Church broke ground for an expansion of the building. The expansion was planned to include a new sanctuary to accommodate 465 worshippers. During the construction, church members worshiped at the Western Springs Christian Reformed Church which rescheduled its own services to accommodate the Baptist congregants. The church had 210 members in 2001. (Photo courtesy of Betsy J. Green.)

The Christian Reformed Church at 5140 Wolf Rd. began with a small congregation in 1935. The present church building was completed in 1959. In 1964, an education wing was added to provide space for meetings, study groups, and social events. The church celebrated its 50th anniversary in 1985. Church membership in 2001 was about 500. (Photo courtesy of Betsy J. Green.)

The First Congregational Church of Western Springs (1106 Chestnut St.) celebrated its 100th anniversary in 1987. The church membership grew from 21 members in 1887 to 1,175 members in 2001. The 1929 church building was designed by noted Prairie School architect George Grant Elmslie, who was once an associate of Louis Sullivan. (Photo courtesy of Betsy J. Green.)

This photo of the Grace Evangelical Lutheran Church at 4101 Wolf Rd. shows the church as it appeared c. 1970. Few changes have been made to the building since it was built in 1952. The congregation formed in 1925, and had formerly worshiped in a building that occupied the southeast corner of Central and Burlington avenues in 2001.

In 2001, the Grace Evangelical Lutheran Church appeared the same as it always has. The church celebrated its 75th anniversary in 2000 with several events including a reunion of people who had been confirmed at the church. The church had 243 members in 2001. (Photo courtesy of Betsy J. Green.)

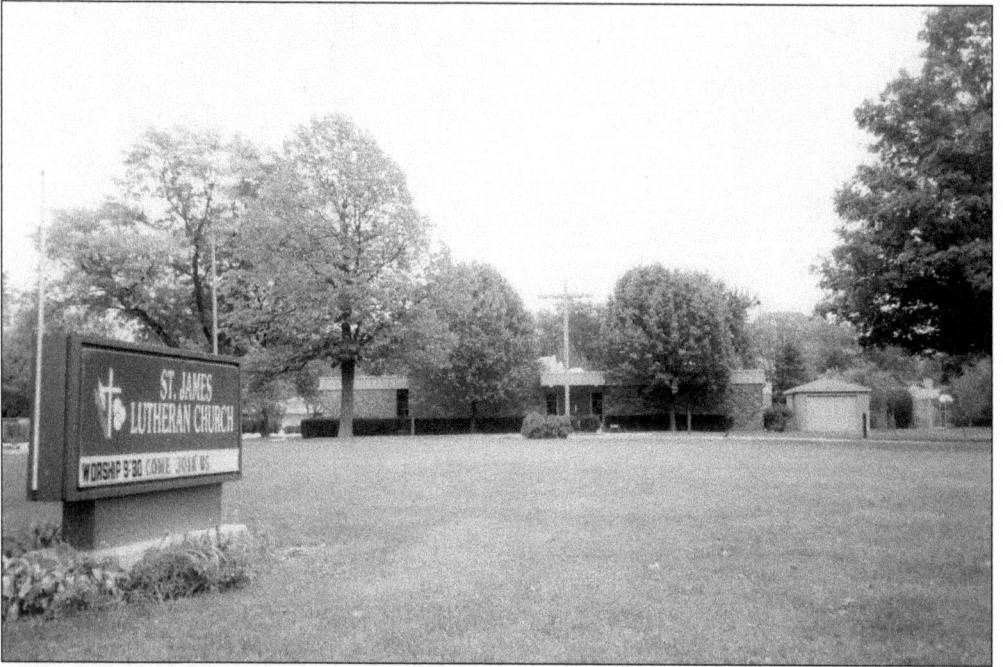

Saint James Lutheran Church at 5129 Wolf Rd. was founded in 1957. The construction of the church was completed in 1960. The church celebrated its 40th anniversary in 1997 with a special service at the Forest Hills School. In 2000, the congregation buried a time capsule to be opened in 2025. The membership in 2001 stood at 168. (Photo courtesy of Betsy J. Green.)

The former Swedish Methodist Church at 1215 Chestnut St. was built in 1893 by Charles Gustafson for the Swedish-speaking congregation which had formed in 1888. It served the Swedish population of the village until 1949. The church building was sold to the Masonic Lodge who still used it for meetings in 2001.

The First United Methodist Church building (4300 Howard Ave.) was built in 1951. The congregation celebrated its centennial in 1988. In 2001, the church was used by several community groups including an exercise class, Indian Princesses and Indian Guides, Cub Scouts, the West Suburban Garden Club, and the B.E.D.S. program. B.E.D.S. stands for Building Ecumenical Disciples through Sheltering. The church membership in 2001 was 215. (Photo courtesy of Betsy J. Green.)

The congregation of the Presbyterian Church of Western Springs met for the first time in 1955. Membership numbered 67. The present building at 5250 Wolf Rd. was completed in 1960. There were 353 church members in 2000. (Photo courtesy of Betsy J. Green.)

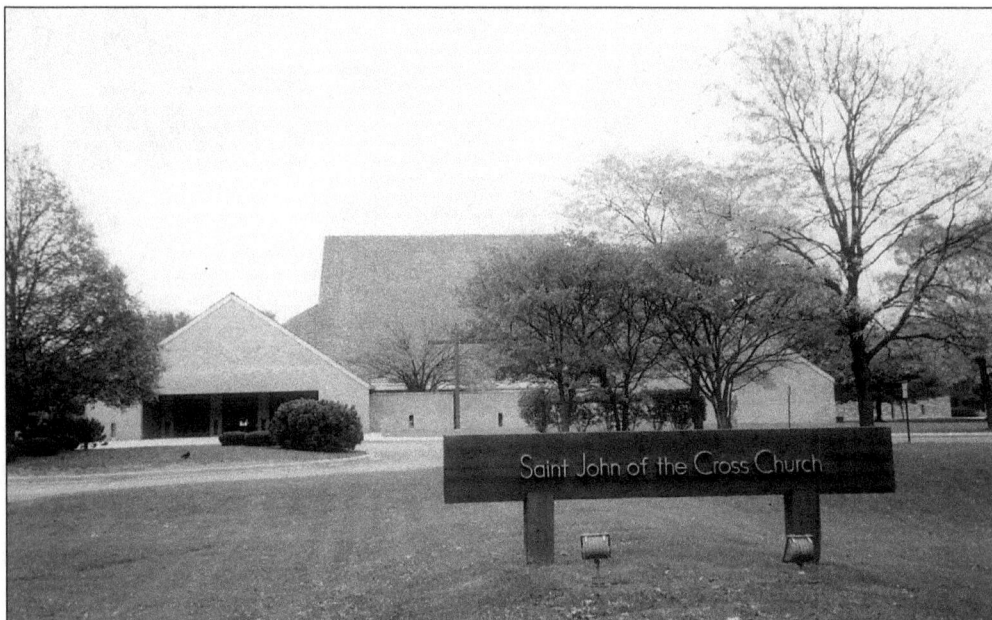

The congregation of the Saint John of the Cross Church held their first mass in 1960 at Lyons Township High School's South Campus. In 1961, the St. John of the Cross School was built and served as both school and church. The church building at 5505 Wolf Rd. was completed in 1976. The church celebrated its 25th anniversary in 1985. In 2001, the church contained 3,830 families. (Photo courtesy of Betsy J. Green.)

The All Saints Episcopal Church building at 4370 Woodland Ave. was built in 1962 on the site of the former Quaker Church. Before that the congregation had worshiped in several places in the village. The congregation celebrated its 100th anniversary in 1994. (Photo courtesy of Betsy J. Green.)

Nine

HOME IS WHERE THE HEART IS

Western Springs has always been known as a community of attractive homes. This chapter focuses on those built in the first half of the 1900s.

Homes built in the decades between 1900 and 1930 tended to be Foursquare, Prairie, Bungalow, or Craftsman style. These styles were smaller and simpler than the late 19th-century houses. These homes were more affordable than Victorian styles and easier to clean. Most of these houses were also built with modern conveniences—electrical wiring, central heat, and indoor plumbing—items that had to be added to 1800s homes.

Although some of these homes were individually designed by architects, many were built from blueprints obtained from plan book companies. Still others were assembled from factory-cut lumber sold by catalog companies such as Sears, Roebuck & Company, and Montgomery Ward.

From the 1920s until the 1950s, four other styles were popular in the village—Tudor Revival, Colonial Revival, Dutch Colonial Revival, and Cape Cod. In the 1950s and 1960s, the most commonly built homes in Western Springs were Ranches and Split Levels.

Older neighborhoods contain a mixture of many different styles of domestic architecture, while it is possible to drive down other streets and pin down the decade in which the street was opened for development.

In the 1990s, there was increasing concern by some residents that the village was losing some of its character as more and more older homes were being demolished to make way for new homes.

A 1920's photo of the beginning of construction of the Forest Hills subdivision echoes the optimistic feeling of that era—"Forging Ahead." A variety of domestic architectural styles were built in Western Springs in the 1900s. This home at the corner of Grand Avenue and 47th Street is an example of the Tudor-Revival style that was popular in the 1920s.

The Foursquare style was popular during the first two decades of the 20th century. Although many of these homes have four rooms on each floor, the name refers to the homes' solid and sturdy appearance. The homes' simple lines were influenced by the Prairie style and the Craftsman (or Arts and Crafts) style. As architectural styles began to become simpler and less expensive, more people were able to afford their own homes. Household help became more expensive, so smaller homes were easier to maintain. After 1900, as many prospective homeowners began to demand expensive modern conveniences (such as indoor plumbing, electricity, and central heat), homes became simpler in order to keep prices reasonable. Foursquare homes are sometimes called "Contractors' Prairie" because they are seen as Prairie-style homes that have been modified to fit on smaller lots. Most Foursquare homes have a hipped roof and horizontal trim.

There was a renewed appreciation for the Bungalow style in the Chicago suburbs in 2001 as the City of Chicago and the Chicago Architecture Foundation focused efforts on preserving the city's bungalows. The Bungalow style has its roots in simple homes in India and also in workingmen's cottages of the late 1800s. Most Bungalows are rectangular and have one and a half stories. Bungalows in Chicago tend to be made of brick, but some were covered with stucco or wood shingles or siding. The floor plans of Bungalows are very similar—the living room was in the front, the kitchen was in the back (you never had to ask where the bathroom was in a bungalow). Little space was dedicated to hallways. Many rooms opened onto other rooms. There were frequently bedrooms on the main floor. The custom of planting bushes or other plants near the foundation of a house originated with bungalows.

The Craftsman style co-existed with Prairie, Foursquare, and Bungalow homes in the early decades of the 1900s, and was the most popular style nationwide from 1905 until the 1920s. The Craftsman style was influenced by the English Arts and Crafts movement of the late 1800s and early 1900s. These one or two-story homes are characterized by low-pitched gable roofs with wide eaves and decorative triangular knee braces beneath them. The roof rafters are often exposed. Porches are common, generally supported by short square columns. In the late 1990s, there was a renewed interest in Craftsman-style homes in part because of the popularity of Arts and Crafts style furniture. Like the Foursquare, Prairie, and Bungalow styles, Craftsman-style homes favor straight square lines over curves or fancy trim. All four styles of home frequently have windows with multiple vertical panes on the top sash, and a single pane on the bottom sash.

Prairie-style homes are not as numerous in the village as are the previous three architectural styles. People may have considered them too modern. Oak Park's Frank Lloyd Wright is the most famous name associated with this style. Prairie-style homes have low-pitched hipped roofs with wide eaves. Horizontal banding under the second-story windows, or contrasting colors on the first and second story, makes the homes appear shorter and closer to the ground. The use of art glass (colored glass) set in geometric patterns is also seen. Bands of vertical windows create a horizontal effect as well. The frequent use of stucco with board trim in Prairie homes is believed to have been a result of Prairie School architects' interest in Japanese architecture. This is in part due to some buildings built by Japanese carpenters at the 1893 Columbian Exhibition (World's Fair) in Chicago.

Tudor Revival-style homes are common in the areas of Western Springs that were developed in the 1920s—the Forest Hills neighborhood and the Field Park area. Characterized by steeply pitched roofs, these homes frequently have chimneys on the front of the house and/or a rounded-top doorway in a gabled entryway.

Dutch Colonial Revival-style homes were another popular style in the village during the 1920s and 1930s. These homes have gambrel roofs, often with shed dormers. The gambrel roof creates more useable room on the second floor.

110

Colonial Revival-style homes were most popular in the 1950s, although the style was still popular in Western Springs at the end of the 20th century. This style is loosely based on styles that were popular on the East Coast before 1776. The interest in American styles of domestic architecture began with the United States Centennial in 1876.

Closely related is the Cape Cod which is sometimes considered a variant of the Colonial Revival style. This style is characterized by dormered windows in a one-and-a-half story home. Colonial Revival homes were often painted gray with white trim, a color scheme that, for most of the 20th century, was mistakenly believed to be authentic colonial colors.

111

French Eclectic-style homes are also found in Western Springs in areas built during the 1920s. Like the picturesque Tudor Revival style, this was also inspired by European domestic architecture. These are some of the few homes in the village to have towers. The towers are generally located on an inner corner of the house.

The 1950s and 1960s saw a return to a simpler form of house—the Ranch. These appear in neighborhoods in the village that were developed during the mid-20th century. Some architectural historians believe that ranches are essentially bungalows that were built parallel to the street.

Another style popular with 1960's builders was the Split Level. The lowest floor was used for the garage, the recreation ("rec") room, and the laundry room. The middle floor held the public areas—the living room, dining room, and kitchen. The upper floor held the private areas—the bedrooms and bathroom.

From 1908 until 1940, Sears Roebuck & Company sold about 100,000 homes by mail. The Sears kit included everything except the tools and the foundation. All the pre-cut boards and other materials (nails, screws, paint, doors, windows, etc.) were shipped by rail. Some Sears' homes were small and some were larger homes such as this attractive *Sherburne* model in Western Springs, which cost less than $3,000. Assembly was required.

Another Sears' catalog home found in the village is this well-preserved *Crescent* model. This was one of the more popular models that Sears sold. The company offered it from 1921 until 1932 for less than $2,500. Sears catalogs showed how the homes would look with Sears' furnishings inside with the expectation that homeowners would also buy these items from the catalog company.

Ten

INTO THE
NEW MILLENNIUM

A s the village of Western Springs entered the 21st century, the village government sent a survey to the residents to learn how the citizens felt about their lifestyle. The railroad was still used by more than two-thirds of the villagers, although fewer than 14 percent used it for daily commuting to work.

A majority of the residents shopped in the downtown each week. Perhaps this is why a majority of Western Springers said that they heard about village news via word of mouth. Although the residents retained such characteristics of small town life, they were by no means living in the past. Three-quarters of the residents who responded to the survey used the Internet in their homes.

Most residents felt that demolishing old houses was not a problem and actually improved the village; however, they felt that many of the new houses were too large in proportion to the lots on which they were built. Many residents wanted the village to further regulate teardowns.

Although Western Springs began its existence as a "dry" village, most villagers in 2001 wanted to have restaurants that served alcohol, and to be able to buy alcohol in supermarkets.

One of the most interesting results on the survey was that more than 12 percent of the residents had once moved out of Western Springs, but later returned to live here. This percentage is statistically high, and indicated that the village is still a place that many people prefer to call "home."

In 1968, the village offices moved to their new space at 740 Hillgrove Ave. (The west side of the building on Wolf Road is shown above.) From 1892 until 1967, the offices had been located on the first and second floors of the water tower. (Photo courtesy of Betsy J. Green.)

Since its construction in 1892, the Western Springs Water Tower has been a visible symbol of the stability of the village. The water tower was listed on the National Register of Historic Places in 1981. Its appearance is virtually unchanged since it was built, and it is one of the few municipal water towers that also housed the offices of local government. In 2001, it was the only building in the village that was listed on the NRHP. It housed the collections of the Western Springs Historical Society on the first and second floors. The third floor was converted to a children's museum in 1995. The photos in this chapter were taken in the fall of 2001. Many American flags were being flown in public and private spaces in Western Springs and the United States at that time. The flags were flown in memory of the thousands of people who were killed by terrorists in New York, Pennsylvania, and Washington D.C. on September 11, 2001. (Photo courtesy of Betsy J. Green.)

The Grand Avenue Community Center at 4211 Grand Ave. was formerly the Grand Avenue School. In 2001, the building housed a daycare center, a drop-in center for senior citizens, the archives of the Western Springs Historical Society, and provided rehearsal spaces for musicians, dancers, and theater groups. (Photo courtesy of Betsy J. Green.)

This building at 800 Chestnut St. has housed the Thomas Ford Memorial Library since it was built in 1932. As the community grew, so did the library. In 1952 the building was enlarged, and again in 1992. At the end of the 20th century, the library added personal computers for library patrons who did not have Internet access in their homes. (Photo courtesy of Betsy J. Green.)

The south campus of Lyons Township High School opened at 4900 S. Willow Springs Rd. in 1956. Freshman and sophomores attended this campus. Juniors and seniors attended the north campus in La Grange. The high school celebrated its 100th anniversary in 1988. In 2001, there were 3,441 students enrolled on both campuses. (Photo courtesy of Betsy J. Green.)

The John Laidlaw School at 4072 Forest Ave. was built at the midpoint of the 20th century (in 1950). An addition in 1998 accommodated an increase in the number of students and the need for more space for the learning center that housed computers and library books. In 2001, there were 416 students at Laidlaw, divided into three classes of students for each grade, kindergarten through fifth grade. (Photo courtesy of Betsy J. Green.)

Another mid-century school was Forest Hills School at 5020 Central Ave., built in 1953. The school had 262 students in 2001 in grades kindergarten through fifth. In the summer of 2001, major renovations made to the school included upgrades to the library and computer rooms. The school will celebrate its 50th anniversary in 2003. (Photo courtesy of Betsy J. Green.)

The McClure Junior High School at 4225 Wolf Rd. is the oldest school building in Western Springs that is still being used as a public school. It is not surprising that this building has changed the most (see a vintage photo of the school in chapter 2). The main entrance, part of a 1990's addition, faced Johnson Avenue in 2001. There were 455 students in grades six through eight. (Photo courtesy of Betsy J. Green.)

Field Park Elementary School at 4335 Howard Ave. was built in 1952. This school, along with Laidlaw and Forest Hills, was built to accommodate the "baby boomers" who were born in the post World War II years. All the public schools in Western Springs added space in the 1990s to accommodate the increased number of children in the village. Forest Hills had 256 students in 2001. (Photo courtesy of Betsy J. Green.)

St. John of the Cross School opened in 1961 and originally housed the school and church. The church was completed in 1976. In 2001, the school broke ground for an addition that was scheduled to be completed in 2004. The school contained 781 students in grades K through 8 in the fall of 2001. (Photo courtesy of Betsy J. Green.)

Ever since the village was settled, Western Springs residents have used well water, even though many neighboring communities obtained their water from Lake Michigan. The Water Department's water treatment plant at 614 Hillgrove Ave. began operating in 1932. In 2001, approximately 400,000,000 gallons of water were softened and purified here. (Photo courtesy of Betsy J. Green.)

In 1954, the Western Springs Service Club (also called the Western Springs Swimming Pool) at 1300 Hillgrove Ave. opened its doors to members. It was built on land that was formerly owned by Vaughan's Seed Company. Both the pools and the building had a major renovation in 1996. (Photo courtesy of Betsy J. Green.)

The Western Springs Law Enforcement Group occupied the southeastern corner of the Village Municipal Building at 740 Hillgrove Ave. In 2001, in addition to law enforcement, the group's services included bike patrol officers, safety education, supplying animal traps, and conducting the D.A.R.E. (Drug Abuse Resistance Education) and V.E.G.A. (Violence Education and Gang Awareness) programs. (Photo courtesy of Betsy J. Green.)

The Western Springs firehouse was built in 1968 after having occupied several locations in the village. Two main branches of the village government were located the building in 2001—the Department of Fire and Emergency Medical Services, and the Department of Code Enforcement. There were approximately 45 men and women who worked for the Fire Department in 2001. (Photo courtesy of Betsy J. Green.)

In 1997, the Western Springs Recreation Department moved into its own building at 1500 Walker St. Formerly housed in the former Clark School and the Grand Avenue School, the department's new location included a larger gym, and classrooms for child care, dance classes, aerobics classes, and other activities. (Photo courtesy of Betsy J. Green.)

Constructed in 1967 in the same Colonial Revival architectural style as the village offices, the Western Springs Post Office was located at 4479 Lawn Ave. in 2001. In the 1990s, a wheelchair ramp was added to the front of the building to facilitate access to the building. In the fall of 2001, it cost 34¢ to send a one-ounce first-class letter. (Photo courtesy of Betsy J. Green.)

The Theatre of Western Springs' brick building at 4384 Hampton Ave. was completed in 1961, and a second smaller theater was added to the building in 1976. The 73rd season in 2001-2 included *The Last Night of Ballyhoo*, *Top Girls*, *As Bees in Honey Drown*, *A Murder is Announced*, *The Importance of Being Ernest*, *Dearly Departed*, *Tartuffe*, and *A Christmas Carol*. (Photo courtesy of Betsy J. Green.)

The village's third train station at 914 Burlington Ave. was built in 1972. It was still standing in 2001, although there were discussions in the village that year about building a new station west of the downtown area. In 2001, the tracks were used by the Burlington Northern Santa Fe railroad. (Photo courtesy of Betsy J. Green.)

The business area of Western Springs parallels the railroad tracks. Hillgrove Avenue is named for a small hill that once stood north of the tracks in La Grange. The building at 808 Hillgrove Ave. may be one of the oldest one in the downtown area. In 2001, the Spaghetti Bowl Restaurant was located at this address. Other businesses on the block that stretched from Wolf Road to Lawn Avenue included: 800—Western Springs Automotive, 810—Christopher English & Associates, Western Springs Federal Credit Union, On-The-Spot Massage Therapy, 812—Grant Dixon & Sons Realtors, 814—The Competitive Foot, 816—2-B Weavers, 818—Eileen Hare Interiors, 820—Dixon Realtors, 822—Edward Jones Investments, R.J. Walsh & Associates, Allstate Insurance Corp., and 824—American Homes Real Estate. (Photo courtesy of Betsy J. Green.)

Burlington Avenue is named for the Chicago, Burlington & Quincy Railroad that runs through the main business area of the village. This street is located about 10 feet above the railroad. In the 1930s, there was a suggestion that the tracks be lowered even further so that trains would not interfere with traffic, but this was not done. One of the longest blocks in the business area is Burlington Avenue where it stretches from Wolf Road to Grand Avenue. Businesses located on this block in 2001 included: 801—Kavooras & Bouzios C.PA., 805—Odegaard's Laundry & Cleaners, 807—The Creative Door, 811—Jon Warren's Hair Salon, 813—The Shoe Corral, 819 RE/Max Properties, 821—Legacies & Lace, 823A—Amlings Flowerland, 823—Changing Seasons, 825 Kirschbaum's Bakery, and 835—Village True Value Hardware. (Photo courtesy of Betsy J. Green.)

The block of Burlington Avenue that stretches from Grand Avenue to Woodland Avenue is directly south of the train station. The train station has been in this location since 1891. Before that, the station was on Hillgrove Avenue, north of the tracks between Wolf Road and Lawn Avenue. The original station burned in 1891 in spite of a well-intentioned bucket brigade. Businesses on this block in 2001 included: 901-03—Harris Bank Western Springs, 907—Leber Jeweler, 909—Snackers Café, 911-15—Casey's Market, 917—The Cottage Collection, 919— Stems and Twigs, 921—Kings & Queens Gift Garden, 923—Dye Hard Salon, 925—Western Springs Fruit Store, and 929—Oberweis Dairy. In addition to the businesses listed on Hillgrove and Burlington Avenues, there are residential apartments above some businesses. (Photo courtesy of Betsy J. Green.)

One of the most controversial issues that occupied the residents of Western Springs in the last decade of the 20th century was that of "teardowns." The trend of demolishing smaller, older homes and replacing them with much larger homes was first noted in the neighboring village of Hinsdale. Soon, teardowns were happening in Western Springs. This home was demolished in the mid-1990s. (Photo courtesy of Jeanette Fanta.)

While some Western Springs residents objected to the disappearance of attractive and affordable older homes, other families felt that existing homes did not fit their lifestyle and that new larger homes were an improvement. In 2001, about 24 homes were demolished in the village, and replaced with larger homes. (Photo courtesy of Betsy J. Green.)

Visit us at
arcadiapublishing.com

www.ingramcontent.com/pod-product-compliance
Lightning Source LLC
Chambersburg PA
CBHW050611110426
42813CB00008B/2522